PRENTICE HALL **A/B**

Practice Workbook

D0565586

PEARSON

Prentice
Hall

Boston, Massachusetts
Upper Saddle River, New Jersey

30   17
ISBN 0-13-036000-7

Realidades A/B

Para empezar

En la escuela

Nombre _____

Fecha _____

Hora _____

Practice Workbook **P–1**

¿Cómo te llamas?

It is the first day of school in Madrid, and students are getting to know each other. Complete the dialogues by circling the appropriate words and phrases.

1. A: ¡Hola! (Hasta luego. / ¿Cómo te llamas?)

    B: Me llamo Rubén. ¿Y tú?

    A: Me llamo Antonio.

    B: (Mucho gusto. / Bien, gracias.)

    A: Igualmente, Rubén.

2. It is 9:00 in the morning.

    A: (¡Buenas tardes! / ¡Buenos días!) ¿Cómo te llamas?

    B: Buenos días. Me llamo Rosalía. ¿Cómo te llamas tú?

    A: Me llamo Enrique. (¿Cómo estás, Rosalía? / Gracias, Rosalía.)

    B: Muy bien, gracias. ¿Y tú?

    A: (Encantado. / Bien.)

    B: Adiós, Enrique.

    A: (¡Sí! / ¡Nos vemos!)

3. It is now 2:00 P.M.

    A: ¡Buenas tardes, Sr. Gómez!

    B: (¡Buenas noches! / ¡Buenas tardes!) ¿Cómo te llamas?

    A: Me llamo Margarita.

    B: Mucho gusto, Margarita.

    A: (Buenos días. / Encantada.) ¡Adiós, Sr. Gómez!

    B: (¡Hasta luego! / ¡Bien!)

Realidades A/B

Nombre _____

Hora _____

Para empezar

Fecha _____

Practice Workbook **P–2**

En la escuela

¿Eres formal o informal?

A. Circle the phrases below that can be used to talk to teachers. Underline the phrases that can be used to talk to other students. Some phrases may be both circled and underlined.

¡Hola!	¿Cómo está Ud.?	Mucho gusto.	¿Qué tal?
Buenos días.	¿Cómo estás?	¿Y usted?	¡Hasta luego!
¡Nos vemos!	Buenos días, señor.	Estoy bien.	¿Y tú?

B. Circle **Ud.** or **tú** to indicate how you would address the person being spoken to.

1. "Hola, Sr. Gómez."   **Ud.**   **Tú**

2. "¿Qué tal, Luis?"   **Ud.**   **Tú**

3. "¿Cómo estás, Paco?"   **Ud.**   **Tú**

4. "¡Buenos días, profesor!"   **Ud.**   **Tú**

5. "Adiós, señora."   **Ud.**   **Tú**

C. Number the following phrases from 1–5 to create a logical conversation. Number 1 should indicate the first thing that was said, and 5 should indicate the last thing that was said.

_____ Bien, gracias, ¿y Ud.?

_____ ¡Hasta luego!

_____ Buenas tardes.

_____ ¡Buenas tardes! ¿Cómo está Ud.?

_____ Muy bien. ¡Adiós!

Realidades A/B

Para empezar

En la escuela

Nombre _____

Hora _____

Fecha _____

Practice Workbook **P–3**

Por favor

Your Spanish teacher has asked you to learn some basic classroom commands. Write the letter of the appropriate phrase next to the picture it corresponds to.

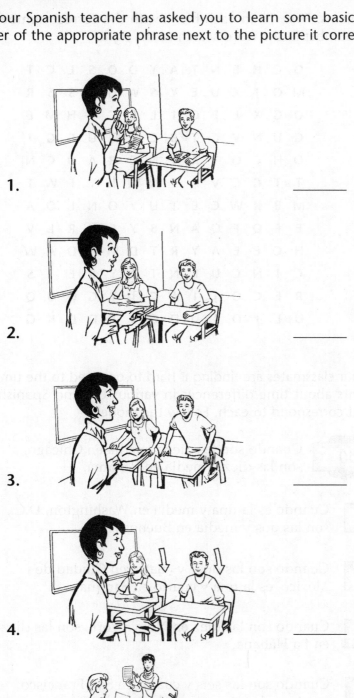

1. _____

2. _____

3. _____

4. _____

5. _____

A. Saquen una hoja de papel.

B. Siéntense, por favor.

C. Repitan, por favor.

D. ¡Silencio, por favor!

E. Levántense, por favor.

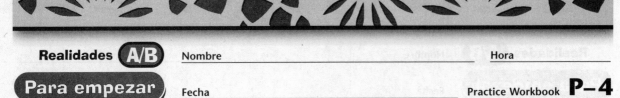

Realidades A/B

Para empezar

En la escuela

Nombre _____

Fecha _____

Hora _____

Practice Workbook **P–4**

Los números

A. Here are some simple math problems. First, fill in each blank with the correct number. Then, find the Spanish word for that number in the word search to the right.

1. $7 \times 8 =$ _____

2. 50, 40, _____ , 20, 10 . . .

3. $75 + 7 =$ _____

4. 55, 60, 65, _____ , 75, 80 . . .

5. 97, 98, 99, _____ . . .

6. $24 \div 2 =$ _____

7. 72, 60, _____ , 36, 24 . . .

```
O C H E N T A Y D O S L C T
M O J X U E Y S W H U S S R
O G X L E G I L E C E H M E
G U N V C T B C R T U C G I
O H C O Y A T N E R A U C N
T T C C V A T N W L Y F W T
M B K W C E T U Y O N L O A
E F Q F Q A N B Y F K R L V
H C E E A Y R T D M W D A W
C I N C U E N T A Y S E I S
R E C O J I W C J Y G Q U Q
U L J D I U D G V X D D K G
```

B. As exchange students, you and your classmates are finding it hard to get used to the time difference. Below are some statements about time differences in various U.S and Spanish-speaking cities. Write in the times that correspond to each. Follow the model.

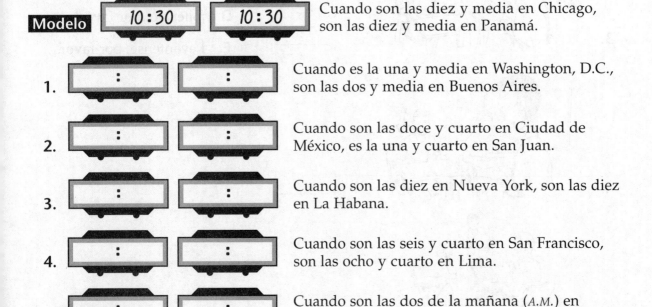

Modelo `10:30` `10:30` Cuando son las diez y media en Chicago, son las diez y media en Panamá.

1. Cuando es la una y media en Washington, D.C., son las dos y media en Buenos Aires.

2. Cuando son las doce y cuarto en Ciudad de México, es la una y cuarto en San Juan.

3. Cuando son las diez en Nueva York, son las diez en La Habana.

4. Cuando son las seis y cuarto en San Francisco, son las ocho y cuarto en Lima.

5. Cuando son las dos de la mañana (*A.M.*) en Madrid, son las siete de la tarde (*P.M.*) en Bogotá.

Go Online WEB CODE jcd-0002 **PHSchool.com**

Realidades A/B

Para empezar

En la escuela

Nombre _____

Fecha _____

Hora _____

Practice Workbook **P–5**

El cuerpo

A. You are watching your neighbor's toddler Anita for a few hours after school. She is playing with her **muñequita** (*doll*) Chula and is practicing words to identify body parts. Help her by drawing lines to connect her doll's body parts with their correct names.

el ojo
la boca
el dedo
el estómago
la nariz
la mano
el brazo
el pie
la cabeza
la pierna

B. Now write three sentences using the phrase **me duele** and body parts.

1. _____

2. _____

3. _____

Realidades A/B

Para empezar

En la clase

Nombre _____

Fecha _____

Hora _____

Practice Workbook **P–6**

Combinaciones

A. Write the correct article (**el** or **la**, or both) before each of the items below.

1. _____ bolígrafo

2. _____ lápiz

3. _____ sala de clases

4. _____ profesora

5. _____ cuaderno

6. _____ carpeta

7. _____ profesor

8. _____ estudiante

9. _____ pupitre

10. _____ hoja de papel

B. To make sure that there are enough school supplies for everyone, your teacher has asked you to help take inventory. Complete each sentence by writing the name and number of each item pictured. Follow the model.

Modelo   veinticinco   No hay un ____*libro*____. Hay __25__.

1. sesenta y siete   No hay un _____. Hay _____.

2. cien   No hay un _____. Hay _____.

3. veintidos   No hay un _____. Hay _____.

4. diecinueve   No hay un _____. Hay _____.

5. treinta y seis   No hay un _____. Hay _____.

Go Online WEB CODE jcd-0004
PHSchool.com

El calendario

February has just ended on a leap year. Because of this, Pepe is completely lost in planning out March. Help him get his days straight by using the calendar. Follow the model.

lunes	martes	miércoles	jueves	viernes	sábado	domingo
				1	2	3
4	5	6	7	8	9	10
11	12	13	14	15	16	17
18	19	20	21	22	23	24
25	26	27	28	29	30	31

Modelo TÚ: Hoy es el cinco de marzo.
PEPE: ¿Es jueves?
TÚ: No, es martes.

1. TÚ: Hoy es el treinta de marzo.
PEPE: ¿Es lunes?
TÚ: _____

2. TÚ: Hoy es el trece de marzo.
PEPE: ¿Es domingo?
TÚ: _____

3. TÚ: Hoy es el veintiuno de marzo.
PEPE: ¿Es domingo?
TÚ: _____

4. TÚ: Hoy es el once de marzo.
PEPE: ¿Es miércoles?
TÚ: _____

5. TÚ: Hoy es el primero de marzo.
PEPE: ¿Es martes?
TÚ: _____

6. TÚ: Hoy es el doce de marzo.
PEPE: ¿Es sábado?
TÚ: _____

7. TÚ: Hoy es el veinticuatro de marzo.
PEPE: ¿Es viernes?
TÚ: _____

8. TÚ: Hoy es el diecisiete de marzo.
PEPE: ¿Es lunes?
TÚ: _____

Realidades **A/B**

Nombre _____

Hora _____

Para empezar

Fecha _____

Practice Workbook **P–8**

En la clase

La fecha

A. Write out the following dates in Spanish. The first one is done for you.

Día/Mes

2/12   *el dos de diciembre* _____

9/3   _____

5/7   _____

4/9   _____

8/11   _____

1/1   _____

¿Recuerdas?

Remember that when writing the date in Spanish, the day precedes the month.

- 19/12 = el 19 de diciembre = December 19
- 27/3 = el 27 de marzo = March 27

B. Now, answer the following questions about dates in complete sentences.

1. ¿Cuál es la fecha de hoy?

_____

2. ¿El Día de San Valentín es el trece de enero?

_____

3. ¿Cuál es la fecha del Año Nuevo?

_____

4. ¿La Navidad (*Christmas*) es el 25 de noviembre?

_____

5. ¿Cuál es la fecha del Día de San Patricio?

_____

6. ¿Cuál es la fecha del Día de la Independencia?

_____

7. ¿Cuál es la fecha de mañana?

_____

Realidades A/B

Para empezar

El tiempo

Nombre _____

Fecha _____

Hora _____

Practice Workbook **P–9**

¿Qué tiempo hace?

You and several Spanish-speaking exchange students are discussing the weather of your home countries.

A. Fill in the chart with the missing information for the area in which you live.

Meses	Estación	Tiempo
diciembre enero _____	_____	_____
marzo _____ _____	_____	_____
junio _____ _____	verano	_____
_____ _____ noviembre	_____	hace viento, hace sol

B. Complete the dialogues below with information from the chart.

1. PROFESORA: ¿Qué tiempo hace en julio?

   ESTUDIANTE: _____

2. PROFESORA: ¿En enero hace calor?

   ESTUDIANTE: _____

3. PROFESORA: ¿En qué meses hace frío?

   ESTUDIANTE: _____

4. PROFESORA: ¿Qué tiempo hace en el verano?

   ESTUDIANTE: _____

5. PROFESORA: ¿Nieva en agosto?

   ESTUDIANTE: _____

Go Online
PHSchool.com WEB CODE jcd-0006

Realidades **A/B**

Para empezar

Nombre _____

Fecha _____

Hora _____

Practice Workbook **P–10**

Repaso

Fill in the crossword puzzle with the Spanish translation of the English words given below.

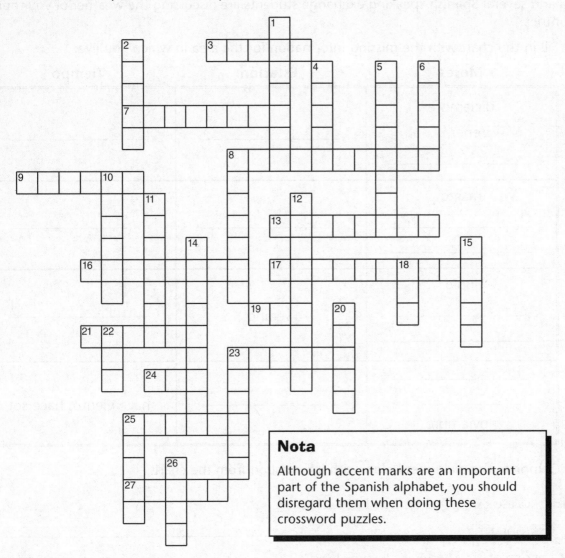

Nota

Although accent marks are an important part of the Spanish alphabet, you should disregard them when doing these crossword puzzles.

Across

3. pencil
7. season
8. See you later!
9. it is raining
13. it is cold
16. winter
17. September
19. day

21. head
23. madam, Mrs.
24. foot
25. week
27. fall

Down

1. Friday
2. Monday
4. it is snowing
5. male teacher
6. January
8. it is sunny
10. summer
11. desk

12. it is hot
14. spring
15. the date
18. month
20. arm
22. year
23. Saturday
25. sir, Mr.
26. Hello

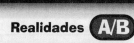
Organizer

I. Vocabulary

Greetings and good-byes

_____

_____

_____

_____

_____

Classroom objects

_____

_____

_____

_____

_____

Body parts

_____

_____

_____

_____

_____

_____

_____

_____

Words to talk about time

_____

_____

_____

_____

_____

Phrases to talk about names

_____

_____

Forms of address (Formal)

_____

_____

_____

Forms of address (Informal)

_____

Phrases to ask and tell how you feel

_____

_____

_____

_____

Realidades A/B

Para empezar

Nombre _____

Hora _____

Fecha _____

Practice Workbook **P-12**

Days of the week	Months of the year
_____	_____
_____	_____
_____	_____
_____	_____
_____	_____
_____	_____
_____	_____

Seasons

_____

_____

_____

Weather expressions

_____

_____

_____

II. Grammar

1. The word *the* is a definite article in English. The singular definite articles in Spanish

   are _____ and _____ , as in _____ **libro** and _____

   carpeta.

2. Most nouns ending with _____ are masculine. Most nouns ending with

   _____ are feminine.

Go Online WEB CODE jcd-0007
PHSchool.com

La pregunta perfecta

Complete each sentence using the word or phrase that best describes the picture.

1.  ¿Te gusta _____?

2.  A mí me gusta _____.

3.  ¿Te gusta _____?

4.  No me gusta _____. ¿Y a ti?

5. 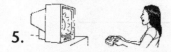 Pues, me gusta mucho _____.

6.  Sí, me gusta mucho _____.

7.  ¿Te gusta mucho _____?

8.  Me gusta _____.

9.  ¡Me gusta mucho _____!

10.  No, ¡no me gusta nada _____!

Go Online
PHSchool.com WEB CODE jcd-0101

A primera vista ▬ *Vocabulario y gramática en contexto* **13**

Realidades **A/B**

Capítulo 1A

Nombre _____

Hora _____

Fecha _____

Practice Workbook **1A–2**

¿A ti también?

Several friends are talking at the bus stop about what they like and do not like to do. Based on the pictures, write the activity that the first person likes or does not like to do. Then, complete the second person's response. Make sure to use **también** or **tampoco** when expressing agreement and disagreement.

1.

ENRIQUE: A mí me gusta mucho _____.
¿A ti te gusta?

DOLORES: Sí, _____.

2.

PABLO: Me gusta _____
¿A ti te gusta?

MARTA: No, _____.

3.

JAIME: No me gusta _____.
¿A ti te gusta?

JULIO: No, _____.

4.

MARÍA: Me gusta _____
¿A ti te gusta?

JULIA: No _____.

5.

CARMEN: No me gusta nada _____.
¿A ti te gusta?

JOSEFINA: Sí, _____.

6.

ROBERTO: Me gusta _____
¿A ti te gusta?

PEDRO: Sí, _____.

Go Online
PHSchool.com
WEB CODE
jcd-0101

Realidades **A/B**

Capítulo 1A

Nombre _____

Hora _____

Fecha _____

Practice Workbook **1A–3**

¿Te gusta o no te gusta?

You are talking to some new students about the things that they like to do. Using the drawings and the model below, complete the following mini-conversations.

Modelo

—¿Te gusta *hablar por teléfono*?

—*Sí, me gusta mucho.*

—¿Te gusta *nadar*?

—*No, no me gusta nada.*

1. —¿Te gusta _____ ?

— _____ .

2. —¿Te gusta _____ ?

— _____ .

3. —¿Te gusta _____ ?

— _____ .

4. —¿Te gusta _____ ?

— _____ .

5. —¿Te gusta _____ ?

— _____ .

6. —¿Te gusta _____ ?

— _____ .

Go Online
PHSchool.com
WEB CODE jcd-0102

A primera vista — *Videohistoria* **15**

Realidades (A/B)

Capítulo 1A

Nombre _____

Fecha _____

Hora _____

Practice Workbook **1A–4**

¿Qué te gusta hacer?

Complete the dialogues below to find out what activities these friends like and dislike.

1. MIGUEL: ¿Te gusta ir a la escuela?

RITA: Sí. _____ mucho ir a la escuela.

¿Y _____?

MIGUEL: Sí, a mí me gusta _____ también. No me gusta

_____ ver la tele _____ jugar videojuegos.

RITA: _____ tampoco.

2. JUAN: No _____ patinar.

PAULA: _____ tampoco. Me gusta leer revistas.

JUAN: ¿_____ más, trabajar o

_____ ?

PAULA: _____ hablar por teléfono.

JUAN: Sí. A mí _____ .

3. AMELIA: A mí _____ pasar tiempo con mis amigos.

CARLOS: A mí me gusta _____ también.

AMELIA: ¿Te gusta trabajar?

CARLOS: No, _____ .

AMELIA: _____ tampoco.

Go Online WEB CODE jcd-0102
PHSchool.com

El infinitivo

Decide what infinitive each picture represents. Then, based on its ending, write the verb in the appropriate column. Use the model as a guide.

	-ar	**-er**	**-ir**
Modelo	_patinar_	_____	_____
1.	_____	_____	_____
2.	_____	_____	_____
3.	_____	_____	_____
4.	_____	_____	_____
5.	_____	_____	_____
6.	_____	_____	_____
7.	_____	_____	_____
8.	_____	_____	_____

Realidades A/B

Capítulo 1A

Nombre _____

Hora _____

Fecha _____

Practice Workbook **1A–6**

Las actividades en común

Cristina is feeling very negative. Using the pictures to help you, write Cristina's negative responses to Lola's questions. Use the model to help you.

Modelo

LOLA: _¿Te gusta patinar?_ _____

CRISTINA: _No, no me gusta nada patinar._ _____

1.

LOLA: _____

CRISTINA: _____

2.

LOLA: _____

CRISTINA: _____

3.

LOLA: _____

CRISTINA: _____

4.

LOLA: _____

CRISTINA: _____

5.

LOLA: _____

CRISTINA: _____

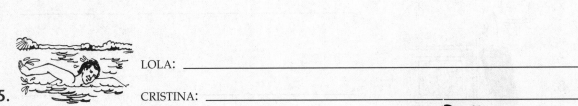

WEB CODE jcd-0104
PHSchool.com

Realidades A/B

Capítulo 1A

Nombre _____

Hora _____

Fecha _____

Practice Workbook **1A–7**

La conversación completa

At lunch, you overhear a conversation between Sara and Graciela, who are trying to decide what they would like to do after school today. Since it is noisy in the cafeteria, you miss some of what they say. Read the conversation through to get the gist, then fill in the missing lines with what the friends probably said.

GRACIELA: ¿Qué te gusta hacer?

SARA: _____ .

GRACIELA: ¿Nadar? Pero es el invierno. ¡Hace frío!

SARA: Sí. Pues, también _____ .

GRACIELA: Pero hoy es martes y no hay programas buenos en la tele.

SARA: Pues, ¿qué _____ hacer a ti?

GRACIELA: _____ .

SARA: ¡Uf! Hay un problema. No me gusta ni jugar videojuegos ni usar la computadora.

GRACIELA: Hmm . . . ¿_____ ?

SARA: No, _____ nada patinar.

GRACIELA: ¿Te gusta bailar o cantar?

SARA: No, _____ .

GRACIELA: Pues, ¿qué _____ , Sara?

SARA: _____ hablar por teléfono.

GRACIELA: ¡A mí también! ¿Cuál es tu número de teléfono?

Realidades A/B

Capítulo 1A

Nombre _____

Hora _____

Fecha _____

Practice Workbook **1A–8**

Repaso

Fill in the crossword puzzle below with the actions indicated by the pictures.

Down

2.

4.

7.

8.

11.

12.

Across

1.

3.

5.

6.

9.

10.

13.

14.

Realidades A/B

Capítulo 1A

Nombre _____

Fecha _____

Hora _____

Practice Workbook **1A–9**

Organizer

I. Vocabulary

Activities I like to do

_____

_____

_____

_____

_____

Activities I may not like to do

_____

_____

_____

_____

_____

Words to say what I like to do

_____

_____

_____

Words to say what I don't like to do

_____

_____

_____

Words to ask what others like to do

_____

_____

_____

_____

II. Grammar

1. The infinitive in English is expressed by writing the word _____ before a verb. In Spanish the infinitive is expressed by the verb endings _____ , _____ , and _____ .

2. In order to say that something doesn't happen in Spanish, use the word _____ before the verb.

3. Use the word _____ to agree with someone who likes something. Use the word _____ to agree with someone who dislikes something.

4. If you do not like either of two choices, use the word _____ .

WEB CODE jcd-0107
PHSchool.com

Realidades **A/B**

Capítulo 1B

Nombre _____

Hora _____

Fecha _____

Practice Workbook **1B–1**

¿Cómo es?

At school you see many different types of people. Describe each person you see in the picture by writing the appropriate adjective on the corresponding blank.

1. _____

2. _____

3. _____

4. _____

5. _____

6. _____

7. _____

8. _____

Go Online WEB CODE jcd-0111
PHSchool.com

Realidades A/B

Capítulo 1B

Nombre _____

Fecha _____

Hora _____

Practice Workbook **1B–2**

Un juego de descripción

Each picture below represents a personality trait. Unscramble the word to identify each trait. Write down the trait, and then circle the picture that corresponds to the unscrambled word.

1.   ísiattcar _____

2.   rvoidate _____

3.   ddonaesdreo _____

4.   jadartobaar _____

5.   iacoarsg _____

6.   zeerosap _____

7.   vesrdoaer _____

8.   utoiesdas _____

Realidades A/B

Capítulo 1B

Nombre _____

Hora _____

Fecha _____

Practice Workbook **1B–3**

¿Cómo eres?

Tito is interviewing Jorge and Ana, two new students from Costa Rica. Tito's questions are written below, but most of Jorge's and Ana's answers are missing. Complete their answers, using the model to help you.

Modelo TITO: Ana, ¿eres perezosa?

   ANA: No, _no soy perezosa_____.

1. TITO: Jorge, ¿eres talentoso?

   JORGE: Sí, _____.

2. TITO: Ana, ¿eres estudiosa?

   ANA: Sí, _____.

3. TITO: Jorge, ¿eres desordenado?

   JORGE: No, _____.

4. TITO: Ana, ¿eres deportista?

   ANA: No, _____.

5. TITO: Jorge, ¿eres sociable?

   JORGE: Sí, _____.

6. TITO: Ana, ¿eres paciente?

   ANA: No, _____.

7. TITO: Jorge, ¿eres inteligente?

   JORGE: Sí, _____.

8. TITO: Ana, ¿eres artística?

   ANA: No, _____.

Go Online WEB CODE jcd-0112
PHSchool.com

Realidades A/B

Capítulo 1B

Nombre _____

Fecha _____

Hora _____

Practice Workbook **1B–4**

¿Qué les gusta?

Based on what each person likes to do, write a description of him or her. Follow the model.

Modelo   A Roberto le gusta esquiar.

Roberto es atrevido. _____

1. A Esteban le gusta tocar la guitarra.

   _____

2. A Pedro le gusta hablar por teléfono.

   _____

3. A Claudia le gusta practicar deportes.

   _____

4. A Teresa le gusta estudiar.

   _____

5. A Luz no le gusta trabajar.

   _____

6. A Manuela le gusta ir a la escuela.

   _____

7. A Carmen le gusta pasar tiempo con amigos.

   _____

8. A Lucía le gusta dibujar.

   _____

Realidades **A/B**

Capítulo 1B

Nombre _____

Fecha _____

Hora _____

Practice Workbook **1B–5**

Me gusta . . .

Some new exchange students at your school are introducing themselves. Using the model as a guide, fill in the blanks in their statements with the actions and adjectives suggested by the pictures. Do not forget to use the correct (masculine or feminine) form of the adjective.

Modelo

A mí _me gusta leer_ .

Yo _soy inteligente_ .

1.

A mí _____ .

Yo _____ .

2.

A mí _____ .

Yo _____ .

3.

A mí _____ .

Yo _____ .

4.

A mí _____ .

Yo _____ .

5.

A mí _____ .

Yo _____ .

6.

A mí _____ .

Yo _____ .

Go Online WEB CODE jcd-0114
PHSchool.com

Realidades A/B

Capítulo 1B

Nombre _____

Fecha _____

Hora _____

Practice Workbook **1B–6**

¿Un o una?

A. Look at the drawings below and decide if they represent masculine or feminine words. Then, label the item in the space provided. Don't forget to use the appropriate indefinite article (**un** or **una**).

Modelo _un profesor_

1. _____

2. _____

3. _____

4. _____

5. _____

6. _____

B. Now, look at the drawings below and describe each person. Make sure to use all the words from the word bank. Don't forget to use the correct definite article (**el** or **la**) and to make the adjectives agree with the nouns.

estudiante	familia	chico	chica	profesor	profesora

Modelo _La estudiante_
es trabajadora.

1. _____

2. _____

3. _____

4. _____

5. _____

6. _____

WEB CODE
jcd-0113

Manos a la obra ━ *Gramática* **27**

Realidades A/B

Capítulo 1B

Nombre _____

Fecha _____

Hora _____

Practice Workbook **1B–7**

Oraciones completas

Choose sentence parts from each of the word banks below, then put them in the correct order to form complete sentences. Follow the model.

Subjects:		Verbs:	
Marta	Yo	es soy eres	
El Sr. Brown	Rolando		
La Srta. Moloy	Tú		

Indefinite articles + nouns:		Adjectives:	
un estudiante	una estudiante	reservado(a)	deportista
un chico	un profesor	inteligente	estudioso(a)
una chica	una profesora	perezoso(a)	bueno(a)

Modelo   Yo soy *un chico estudioso.* _____

1. _____

2. _____

3. _____

4. _____

5. _____

6. _____

7. _____

8. _____

9. _____

10. _____

Go Online WEB CODE jcd-0115
PHSchool.com

Realidades A/B

Capítulo 1B

Nombre _____

Fecha _____

Hora _____

Practice Workbook **1B-8**

Repaso

Down

1. según mi ____
2. no paciente
3. no ordenado
5. Un chico/una chica que practica deportes es ____.
6. *I like:* "Me ____."
8.
11. No es trabajador. Es ____.
13.
15.
16. Le gusta pasar tiempo con amigos. Es ____.
18. —¿Cómo ____?
    —Soy sociable.

Across

4.
7. *nice, friendly*
9. no es malo, es ____
10. ¿ ____ se llama?
12.
14.
17.
19.
20.

Repaso del capítulo ▬ *Crucigrama* **29**

Organizer

I. Vocabulary

Words that describe me

_____

_____

_____

_____

_____

Words that may describe others

_____

_____

_____

_____

_____

Words to ask what someone is like

_____

_____

_____

Words to tell what I am like

_____

_____

_____

II. Grammar

1. Most feminine adjectives end with the letter _____. Most masculine adjectives end with the letter _____.

2. Adjectives that can be either masculine or feminine may end with the letters _____ (as in the word _____) or the letter _____ (as in the word _____).

3. The two singular definite articles are _____ and _____. The two singular indefinite articles are _____ and _____.

4. In Spanish, adjectives come (before/after) the nouns they describe.

WEB CODE jcd-0117
PHSchool.com

Realidades A/B

Capítulo 2A

Nombre _____

Fecha _____

Hora _____

Practice Workbook **2A–1**

Las clases

A. Write the name of the item, and the school subject for which you might use it, in the appropriate column below.

¿Qué es?   ¿Para qué clase?

1. _____   1. _____

2. _____   2. _____

3. _____   3. _____

4. _____   4. _____

5. _____   5. _____

6. _____   6. _____

B. Now, unscramble the letters in each word below to find out what classes you have today and what you need to bring to school.

1. éilsgn: la clase de _____

2. trea: la clase de _____

3. ncoridcoiia: el _____

4. zlpiá: el _____

5. aduclcralao: la _____

6. ngtíalceoo: la clase de _____

7. birol: el _____

8. lpsñoea: la clase de _____

9. cámtmeistaa: la clase de _____

10. rteaa: la _____

El horario

You have just received your class schedule. Using the model as a guide, write sentences to describe which classes you have and when you have them.

Horario

Hora	Clase
1	inglés
2	matemáticas
3	arte
4	ciencias sociales
5	el almuerzo
6	tecnología
7	español
8	educación física
9	ciencias naturales

Modelo Tengo _la clase de inglés_ en _la primera hora_ .

1. Tengo _____ en _____ .

2. Tengo _____ en _____ .

3. Tengo _____ en _____ .

4. Tengo _____ en _____ .

5. Tengo _____ en _____ .

6. Tengo _____ en _____ .

7. Tengo _____ en _____ .

8. Tengo _____ en _____ .

Go Online WEB CODE jcd-0201
PHSchool.com

Realidades A/B

Capítulo 2A

Nombre _____

Hora _____

Fecha _____

Practice Workbook **2A–3**

¿Cómo son las clases?

Your friend Marcos is curious about which classes you like and which ones you don't like. Answer his questions using adjectives that you have learned in this chapter. Follow the model.

Modelo	¿Te gusta la clase de matemáticas?

Sí, _es interesante_ .

1. —¿Te gusta la clase de tecnología?

   —Sí, _____ .

2. —¿Te gusta la clase de español?

   —Sí, _____ .

3. —¿Te gusta la clase de matemáticas?

   —No, _____ .

4. —¿Te gusta la clase de ciencias sociales?

   —Sí, _____ .

5. —¿Te gusta la clase de ciencias naturales?

   —No, _____ .

6. —¿Te gusta la clase de educación física?

   —No, _____ .

7. —¿Te gusta la clase de inglés?

   —Sí, _____ .

8. —¿Te gusta la clase de arte?

   —Sí, _____ .

Realidades A/B

Capítulo 2A

Nombre _____

Fecha _____

Hora _____

Practice Workbook **2A–4**

¿Qué necesitas?

You are getting ready for school, and your mother wants to make sure you have everything. Answer her questions according to the model.

Modelo MAMÁ: ¿Tienes la tarea?

TÚ: Sí, _tengo la tarea_____ .

1. MAMÁ: ¿Tienes un libro?

   TÚ: Sí, _____ .

2. MAMÁ: ¿Necesitas una calculadora?

   TÚ: No, _____ .

3. MAMÁ: ¿Tienes una carpeta de argollas para la clase de matemáticas?

   TÚ: No, _____ .

4. MAMÁ: ¿Necesitas un diccionario para la clase de español?

   TÚ: Sí, _____ .

5. MAMÁ: ¿Tienes el cuaderno para la clase de arte?

   TÚ: No, _____ .

6. MAMÁ: ¿Tienes un lápiz?

   TÚ: Sí, _____ .

7. MAMÁ: ¿Necesitas el horario?

   TÚ: No, _____ .

8. MAMÁ: ¿Tienes un bolígrafo?

   TÚ: Sí, _____ .

Realidades A/B

Capítulo 2A

Nombre _____

Hora _____

Fecha _____

Practice Workbook **2A–5**

¡Todo el mundo!

A. How would you talk *about* the following people? Write the correct subject pronoun next to their names. Follow the model.

| Modelo | Marisol | _____ *ella* _____ |

1. Pablo _____

2. María y Ester _____

3. Marta y yo _____

4. Tú y Marisol _____

5. El doctor Smith _____

6. Jorge y Tomás _____

7. Carmen _____

8. Alicia y Roberto _____

9. Rolando y Elena _____

B. How would you talk *to* the following people? Write the correct subject pronoun next to their names. Follow the model.

| Modelo | Tu amiga Josefina | _____ *tú* _____ |

1. El profesor Santiago _____

2. Marta y Carmen _____

3. Anita y yo _____

4. Tu amigo Federico _____

5. La señorita Ibáñez _____

6. Ricardo _____

7. La profesora Álvarez _____

Realidades **A/B**

Capítulo 2A

Nombre _____

Fecha _____

Hora _____

Practice Workbook **2A–6**

El verbo exacto

A. Fill in the chart below with all the forms of the verbs given.

	yo	tú	él/ella/ Ud.	nosotros/ nosotras	vosotros/ vosotras	ellos/ ellas/Uds.
hablar	hablo				habláis	hablan
estudiar				estudiamos	estudiáis	
enseñar		enseñas			enseñáis	
usar					usáis	
necesitar			necesita		necesitáis	

B. Now, fill in the blanks in the following sentences with the correct forms of the verbs in parentheses.

1. Ella _____ inglés. (estudiar)

2. Yo _____ mucho. (bailar)

3. Nosotros _____ por teléfono. (hablar)

4. Ellos _____ la computadora durante la primera hora. (usar)

5. ¿Quién _____ un bolígrafo? (necesitar)

6. Tú _____ en bicicleta mucho, ¿no? (montar)

7. Uds. _____ muy bien en la clase de arte. (dibujar)

8. Nosotras _____ hoy, ¿no? (patinar)

9. El profesor _____ la lección. (enseñar)

10. Ana y María _____ el libro de español. (necesitar)

11. Jaime _____ todos los días. (caminar)

12. Dolores y yo _____. (bailar)

13. Tú y tus amigos _____ muy bien. (cantar)

WEB CODE
jcd-0204

PHSchool.com

Realidades A/B

Capítulo 2A

Nombre _____

Fecha _____

Hora _____

Practice Workbook **2A–7**

¿Qué hacen hoy?

A. Today everyone is doing what he or she likes to do. Follow the model to complete sentences about what everyone is doing.

Modelo   A Luisa le gusta bailar. Hoy _____*ella baila*_____ .

1. A ti te gusta cantar. Hoy _____ .

2. A mí me gusta hablar por teléfono. Hoy _____ .

3. A Francisco le gusta patinar. Hoy _____ .

4. A Ud. le gusta dibujar. Hoy _____ .

5. A Teresa le gusta practicar deportes. Hoy _____ .

B. Using the pictures to help you, tell what everyone is doing today. Follow the model.

Manuel y Carlos

Modelo   Hoy _____*ellos montan en monopatín*_____ .

Amelia y yo

1. Hoy _____ .

tú y Roberto

2. Hoy _____ .

Cristina, Miguel y Linda

3. Hoy _____ .

tú y yo

4. Hoy _____ .

Joaquín y Jaime

5. Hoy _____ .

Sofía y Tomás

6. Hoy _____ .

Realidades Ⓐ/Ⓑ

Capítulo 2A

Nombre _____

Hora _____

Fecha _____

Practice Workbook **2A–8**

Repaso

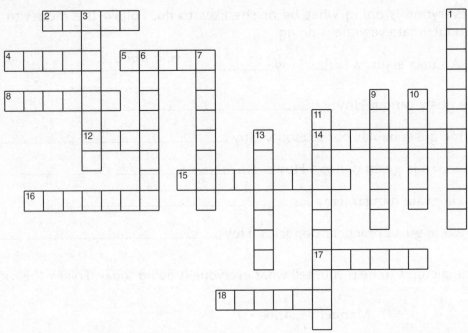

Across ——————————

2. No es difícil. Es ____.

4. la ____ de español

5. *homework*

8. educación ____

12. el ____

14. no divertida

15. **ciencias** ____ : *science*

16. ____, octavo, noveno

17. el ____

18. La profesora ____ la clase.

Down ——————————

1. ____ la ____

3. ____ **sociales**: *social studies*

6. *lunch*

7. carpeta de ____

9. *schedule*

10. cuarta, ____ , sexta

11. la clase de ____

13. primero, segundo, ____

Organizer

I. Vocabulary

Classes I take in school

_____

_____

_____

_____

_____

Words used to refer to people

_____

_____

_____

_____

_____

Words to talk about the order of things

_____

_____

_____

_____

_____

_____

_____

Words to describe my classes

_____

_____

_____

_____

_____

_____

II. Grammar

1. The following are subject pronouns in Spanish: _____ , _____ ,

_____ , _____ , _____ , _____ , _____ ,

_____ , _____ , _____ , _____ , _____ .

2. Use _____ to address someone formally. Use _____ to address someone informally.

3. The **-ar** verb endings are: _____ _____ _____ _____ _____ _____

Now conjugate the verb **hablar**: _____ _____

_____ _____

_____ _____

Realidades **A/B**

Capítulo 2B

Nombre _____

Hora _____

Fecha _____

Practice Workbook **2B–1**

En la clase

Label the items in this Spanish class. Make sure to use the correct definite article (**el** or **la**).

1. _____

2. _____

3. _____

4. _____

5. _____

6. _____

7. _____

8. _____

9. _____

10. _____

11. _____

12. _____

13. _____

Go Online WEB CODE jcd-0211
PHSchool.com

Realidades **A/B**   Nombre _____   Hora _____

Capítulo 2B   Fecha _____   Practice Workbook **2B–2**

¡Mucha confusión!

You come home after school to find a scene of great confusion in your kitchen. Look at the picture, then describe what you see by filling in the blanks in the sentences below with the appropriate words to indicate location.

1. Paquito está _____ del escritorio.

2. Mamá está _____ de la luz (*the light*).

3. Papá está _____ de la ventana.

4. La papelera está _____ de la puerta.

5. Las hojas de papel están _____ de la mesa.

6. Carmen está _____ de la silla.

7. El reloj está _____ de la mesa.

8. El libro está _____ de la silla.

9. El teclado está _____ de la pantalla.

Realidades Ⓐ/Ⓑ

Capítulo 2B

Nombre _____

Fecha _____

Hora _____

Practice Workbook **2B–3**

¿Dónde está?

Rosario is describing the room where she studies to a friend of hers on the phone. Using the picture below, write what she might say about where each item is located. There may be more than one right answer. Follow the model.

Modelo   La mochila está _____encima de la silla_____.

1. El escritorio está _____.

2. La computadora está _____.

3. La papelera está _____.

4. Los disquetes están _____.

5. Una bandera de los Estados Unidos está _____.

6. La silla está _____.

7. El sacapuntas está _____.

8. Los libros de español están _____.

Go Online WEB CODE jcd-0212
PHSchool.com

Realidades A/B

Capítulo 2B

Nombre _____

Hora _____

Fecha _____

Practice Workbook **2B–4**

¿Qué es esto?

Complete the following conversations that you overhear in school.

1. A: ¿_____ estudiantes hay en la clase?

B: _____ veintidós estudiantes en la clase.

2. A: ¿_____?

B: Es la mochila.

3. A: ¿_____ está la computadora?

B: Está allí, al lado de las ventanas.

4. A: ¿_____ una bandera en la sala de clases?

B: Sí, la bandera está allí.

5. A: ¿Dónde están los estudiantes?

B: Los estudiantes _____ la clase de inglés.

6. A: ¿Dónde está el teclado?

B: Está delante _____ la pantalla.

7. A: ¿Dónde está el diccionario?

B: _____ está, debajo del escritorio.

8. A: ¿Qué hay _____ la mochila?

B: Hay muchos libros.

¿Dónde están?

Spanish teachers are conversing in the faculty room. Fill in their conversations using the correct form of the verb **estar**.

1. —¡Buenos días! ¿Cómo _____ Ud., Sra. López?

   —_____ bien, gracias.

2. —¿Dónde _____ Raúl hoy? No _____ en

   mi clase.

   —¿Raúl? Él _____ en la oficina.

3. —Yo no tengo mis libros. ¿Dónde _____?

   —Sus libros _____ encima de la mesa, profesor Martínez.

4. —¿Cuántos estudiantes _____ aquí?

   —Diecinueve estudiantes _____ aquí. Uno

   no _____ aquí.

5. —¿Dónde _____ mi diccionario?

   —El diccionario _____ detrás del escritorio.

6. —¿Cómo _____ los estudiantes hoy?

   —Teresa _____ bien. Jorge y Bernardo _____

   regulares.

7. —Bien, profesores, ¿_____ nosotros listos (*ready*)? Todos los

   estudiantes _____ en la clase.

Realidades A/B

Capítulo 2B

Nombre _____

Fecha _____

Hora _____

Practice Workbook **2B–6**

Muchas cosas

A. Fill in the chart below with singular and plural, definite and indefinite forms of the words given. The first word has been completed.

Definite		Indefinite	
singular	plural	singular	plural
la silla	las sillas	una silla	unas sillas
		un cuaderno	
			unos disquetes
	las computadoras		
la mochila			
			unos relojes
		una bandera	
la profesora			

B. Now, fill in each sentence below with words from the chart.

1. Pablo, ¿necesitas _____ de los Estados Unidos? Aquí está.

2. Marta, ¿tienes _____? ¿Qué hora es?

3. Hay _____ Macintosh en la sala de clases.

4. _____ está en la sala de clases. Ella enseña la clase

   de tecnología.

5. Necesito _____ buena. Tengo muchos libros.

Realidades A/B

Capítulo 2B

Nombre _____

Fecha _____

Hora _____

Practice Workbook **2B–7**

¡Aquí está!

It was a very busy afternoon in your classroom, and things got a little out of order. Write eight sentences describing where things are to help your teacher find everything.

Modelo	*El escritorio está debajo de la computadora* .

1. _____

2. _____

3. _____

4. _____

5. _____

6. _____

7. _____

8. _____

Go Online WEB CODE jcd-0215
PHSchool.com

Realidades (A/B)

Capítulo 2B

Nombre _____

Hora _____

Fecha _____

Practice Workbook **2B–8**

Repaso

Across

2.

5. la ____ de clases

9.

12.

14.

15. La ____ está detrás del pupitre.

16. La computadora está en la ____.

17. *window*

19. *diskette*

20.

Down

1. *pencil sharpener*

3. no está encima de, está ____ de

4.

6.

7. al ____ de: *next to*

8. no delante

10.

11.

13. *mouse*

18. No estás aquí, estás ____.

Repaso del capítulo ● *Crucigrama* **47**

Realidades A/B

Capítulo 2B

Nombre _____ Hora _____

Fecha _____ Practice Workbook **2B–9**

Organizer

I. Vocabulary

Items in my classroom	Words to tell the location of things
_____	_____
_____	_____
_____	_____
_____	_____
_____	_____
_____	_____
_____	_____
_____	_____
_____	
_____	

II. Grammar

1. The forms of **estar** are: _____ _____

   _____ _____

   _____ _____

2. _____ and _____ are the singular definite articles in

   Spanish. Their plurals are _____ and _____ .

3. The singular indefinite articles are _____ and _____ in

   Spanish. Their plurals are _____ and _____ .

Go Online WEB CODE jcd-0216
PHSchool.com

Realidades A/B

Capítulo 3A

Nombre _____

Fecha _____

Hora _____

Practice Workbook **3A–1**

Tus comidas favoritas

You are getting ready to travel as an exchange student to Spain and you are e-mailing your host family your opinions on different foods. Circle the name of the food item that best completes each sentence below.

1. En el desayuno, yo como _____

   a. cereal.   **b.** un sándwich.

2. Mi comida favorita es _____

   a. el té.   **b.** la pizza.

3. Mi fruta favorita es _____

   a. la fresa.   **b.** la sopa.

4. Para beber, yo prefiero _____

   a. los huevos.   **b.** los refrescos.

5. A mí me gusta el jugo de _____

   a. manzana.   **b.** salchicha.

6. En el almuerzo, yo como _____

   a. un sándwich.   **b.** cereal.

7. Cuando hace frío, yo bebo _____

   a. té helado.   **b.** té.

8. Un BLT es un sándwich de verduras con _____

   a. jamón.   **b.** tocino.

9. Cuando voy a un partido de béisbol, yo como _____

   a. la sopa.   **b.** un perrito caliente.

10. En un sándwich, prefiero _____

    a. el queso.   **b.** el yogur.

Realidades A/B

Capítulo 3A

Nombre _____

Fecha _____

Hora _____

Practice Workbook **3A–2**

¿Desayuno o almuerzo?

Your aunt owns a restaurant and is making her breakfast and lunch menus for the day. Help her by writing the foods and beverages that you think she should serve for each meal in the right places on the menus. Some words may be used more than once.

La Casa De Rosalía

El desayuno

comer   beber

La Casa De Rosalía

El almuerzo

comer   beber

Go Online WEB CODE jcd-0301
PHSchool.com

Tus preferencias

You are asking Corazón, an exchange student from Venezuela, about various food items that she likes to eat. Use the pictures to help you complete Corazón's answers. Follow the model.

Modelo

TÚ: ¿Tú comes galletas?

CORAZÓN: No. _Yo como huevos_ .

1.

TÚ: ¿Tú comes salchichas?

CORAZÓN: No. _____.

2.

TÚ: ¿Te gusta más _____ o _____?

CORAZÓN: _____ el café.

3.

TÚ: ¿Tú bebes mucha limonada?

CORAZÓN: No. _____.

4.

TÚ: ¿Tú comes mucha sopa de verduras?

CORAZÓN: No. _____.

5.

TÚ: ¿Tú bebes té helado?

CORAZÓN: No. _____.

6.

TÚ: ¿Tú compartes el desayuno con amigos?

CORAZÓN: No. _____.

Realidades **A/B**

Capítulo 3A

Nombre _____

Fecha _____

Hora _____

Practice Workbook **3A–4**

¿Qué comes?

Carolina, the new exchange student, is having a hard time figuring out the kinds of foods that people like to eat. Answer her questions in complete sentences, using **¡Qué asco!** and **¡Por supuesto!** in at least one answer each.

1. ¿Comes hamburguesas con plátanos?

_____

2. ¿Comes el sándwich de jamón y queso en el almuerzo?

_____

3. ¿Bebes leche en el desayuno?

_____

4. ¿Te gusta la pizza con la ensalada de frutas?

_____

5. ¿Comes papas fritas en el desayuno?

_____

6. ¿Compartes la comida con tu familia?

_____

7. ¿Comes un perro caliente todos los días?

_____

8. ¿Te encantan las galletas con leche?

_____

Go Online WEB CODE jcd-0302
PHSchool.com

Realidades A/B

Capítulo 3A

Nombre _____

Hora _____

Fecha _____

Practice Workbook **3A–5**

El verbo correcto

A. Fill in the chart below with all the forms of the verbs given.

	yo	tú	él/ella/Ud.	nosotros/ nosotras	vosotros/ vosotras	ellos/ ellas/Uds.
comer			*come*		*coméis*	
beber		*bebes*			*bebéis*	
comprender	*comprendo*				*comprendéis*	
escribir				*escribimos*	*escribís*	
compartir					*compartís*	*comparten*

B. Now, using the verbs from Part A, write the missing verb to complete each sentence below.

1. Antonio _____ sus papas fritas con Amelia.

2. Uds. _____ los sándwiches de queso.

3. Yo _____ las salchichas en el desayuno.

4. Nosotros _____ el té helado.

5. Ana _____ la tarea.

6. Tú _____ una carta al profesor.

7. Yo _____ el pan con Jorge.

8. Él _____ jugo de naranja en el desayuno.

9. Nosotros _____ con un lápiz.

10. Paula y Guillermo hablan y _____ español.

11. ¿_____ tú leche en el desayuno?

12. Manolo y Federico _____ las galletas con Susana.

¿Qué te gusta?

A. List your food preferences in the blanks below.

Me gusta	Me gustan	Me encanta	Me encantan
			los sándwiches
_____	_____	_____	_____
_____	_____	_____	_____
			_____

B. Now, organize your preferences into complete sentences. Follow the model.

Modelo   *Me encantan los sándwiches.* _____

1. _____

2. _____

3. _____

4. _____

5. _____

6. _____

7. _____

8. _____

C. Using the words given, write a sentence about each food. Follow the model.

Modelo   El té (encantar) *Me encanta el té* . _____

1. los plátanos (gustar) _____

2. la pizza (encantar) _____

3. las papas fritas (encantar) _____

4. el pan (gustar) _____

WEB CODE jcd-0304
PHSchool.com

Realidades A/B

Capítulo 3A

Nombre _____

Fecha _____

Hora _____

Practice Workbook **3A–7**

Mini-conversaciones

Fill in the blanks in the mini-conversations below with the most logical question or answer.

1. —¿Comparten Uds. el sándwich de jamón y queso?

—Sí, nosotros _____ el sándwich.

2. —¿_____ tú todos los días?

—No, nunca corro. No me gusta.

3. —¿_____ en el desayuno?

—¡Qué asco! No me gustan los plátanos.

4. —¿_____?

—Sí, profesora. Comprendemos la lección.

5. —¿_____?

—Mi jugo favorito es el jugo de manzana.

6. —¿_____?

—Más o menos. Me gusta más la pizza.

7. —¿_____?

—¡Por supuesto! Me encanta el cereal.

Realidades **A/B**

Capítulo 3A

Nombre _____

Fecha _____

Hora _____

Practice Workbook **3A–8**

Repaso

Down ——————————————

2. más o ____

4. ¡Qué ____! No me gustan los guisantes.

5.

6.

7. el té ____

8. las ____ fritas

11. *food*

14.

16. 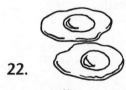 un jugo de ____

17. No como carne. Me gusta la sopa de ____.

19. En los Estados Unidos el ____ es un sándwich y algo de beber.

20. un ____ de naranja

Across ——————————————

1. *always*

3. El Monstruo Comegalletas come muchas ____.

6. el ____ tostado

9. Me gusta el sándwich de jamón y ____.

10.

12.

13. Muchas personas comen cereales con leche en el ____.

15. ¿Te gusta ____ el almuerzo con tus amigos?

18. Me gusta la ____ de frutas, no de lechuga.

21. un yogur de ____

22.

23.

24. el perrito ____

Realidades A/B

Capítulo 3A

Nombre _____

Hora _____

Fecha _____

Practice Workbook **3A–9**

Organizer

I. Vocabulary

Breakfast foods

_____

_____

_____

_____

_____

_____

Lunch foods

_____

_____

_____

_____

_____

_____

Beverages

_____

_____

_____

_____

Words to express likes/dislikes

_____

_____

_____

_____

II. Grammar

1. The **-er** verb endings are: -_____   -_____

   -_____   -_____

   -_____   -_____

   Now conjugate the verb **beber**:   _____   _____

   _____   _____

   _____   _____

2. The **-ir** verb endings are: -_____   -_____

   -_____   -_____

   -_____   -_____

   Now conjugate the verb **compartir**:   _____   _____

   _____   _____

   _____   _____

3. To use **me gusta** and **me encanta** to talk about plural nouns, you add the letter

   _____ to the end of the verb.

WEB CODE jcd-0306
PHSchool.com

Repaso del capítulo ▬ *Vocabulario y gramática*   **57**

Realidades **A/B**

Capítulo 3B

Nombre _____

Hora _____

Fecha _____

Practice Workbook **3B–1**

¡A cenar!

A. You are having a party, and you need to make a shopping list. Write at least three items that you might want to buy under each category. You may use vocabulary from other chapters.

La ensalada de frutas:

_____

_____

_____

_____

_____

Las verduras:

_____

_____

_____

_____

_____

La carne:

_____

_____

_____

_____

_____

Bebemos:

_____

_____

_____

_____

_____

B. Now write three things your guests might like to eat after dinner.

_____

_____

_____

Go Online WEB CODE jcd-0311
PHSchool.com

Realidades A/B

Capítulo 3B

Nombre _____

Fecha _____

Hora _____

Practice Workbook **3B–2**

Más comida

A. Name the most logical food category to which each group of items belongs.

1. el bistec, el pollo, el pescado _____

2. las zanahorias, la cebolla, los guisantes _____

3. las uvas, las manzanas _____

4. el postre, la mantequilla _____

B. Now, answer the following questions logically in complete sentences.

1. ¿Debemos comer las uvas, el helado o los pasteles para mantener la salud?

   _____

2. ¿Es sabrosa la ensalada de frutas con las papas o con los plátanos?

   _____

3. ¿Comemos la mantequilla con el pan tostado o con el bistec?

   _____

4. ¿Bebemos los refrescos o el agua para mantener la salud?

   _____

C. Using the foods below, write sentences telling whether we should or shouldn't eat or drink each thing to maintain good health. Follow the model.

Modelo el agua *Debemos beber el agua para mantener la salud.*

1. los tomates _____

2. las grasas _____

3. los plátanos _____

4. las uvas _____

5. la mantequilla _____

6. la leche _____

Realidades **A/B**

Capítulo 3B

Nombre _____

Fecha _____

Hora _____

Practice Workbook **3B–3**

La respuesta perfecta

You are learning about fitness and nutrition at school, and your friends want to know more. Answer their questions or respond to their statements in complete sentences.

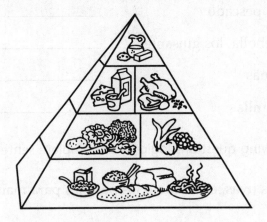

1. ¿Es el tomate bueno para la salud?

   _____

2. ¿Por qué caminas todos los días?

   _____

3. ¿La mantequilla es buena para la salud?

   _____

4. Creo que las grasas son horribles.

   _____

5. ¿Qué debes hacer para mantener la salud?

   _____

6. ¿Prefieres levantar pesas o caminar?

   _____

7. Creo que los espaguetis son sabrosos. ¿Y tú?

   _____

Go Online WEB CODE jcd-0312
PHSchool.com

Realidades A/B

Capítulo 3B

Nombre _____

Hora _____

Fecha _____

Practice Workbook **3B–4**

¿Qué comes?

Angel is asking his friend Estela about foods she likes. Fill in the blanks with the foods suggested by the pictures, then complete Estela's answers.

1. —¿Te gustan _____?

   —No, _____.

2. —¿Prefieres _____ con _____ en el almuerzo o en la cena?

   —_____ en el almuerzo.

3. —¿Te gustan _____?

   —Sí, _____.

4. —¿Prefieres _____ de chocolate o de fruta?

   —_____ de chocolate.

5. —¿Comes _____?

   —Sí, _____.

6. —¿Siempre comes _____ en el almuerzo?

   —No, _____.

7. —¿Te gusta el _____ con _____?

   —Sí, _____.

Realidades A/B

Capítulo 3B

Nombre _____

Fecha _____

Hora _____

Practice Workbook **3B–5**

Las descripciones

A. Fill in the chart below with the singular and plural, masculine and feminine forms of the adjectives given.

Masculine		Feminine	
singular	plural	singular	plural
sabroso			
	prácticos		
		fácil	
	aburridos		
			difíciles
divertido			
		artística	
			buenas
trabajador			

B. Now, complete the sentences below, using some of the words from the chart above. There may be more than one right answer.

1. La ensalada de frutas es _____ para la salud.

2. Me gustan mis clases; son _____.

3. La tarea de matemáticas es _____.

4. Te gustan las computadoras porque son _____.

5. Mi profesor no come pescado porque cree que no es _____.

6. Mis amigos son _____; dibujan muy bien.

7. Tus amigos son muy _____; trabajan mucho.

8. Esquiar y nadar son actividades muy _____.

Go Online WEB CODE jcd-0313
PHSchool.com

Realidades A/B

Nombre _____

Hora _____

Capítulo 3B

Fecha _____

Practice Workbook **3B–6**

¿Cómo son?

Describe the following people using the pictures as clues. Use a form of **ser** plus an adjective. Follow the model.

Modelo

¿Cómo _____es_____ él?

_Él es popular_____.

1. ¿Cómo _____ él?

_____.

2. ¿Cómo _____ ella?

_____.

3. ¿Cómo _____ ellas?

_____.

4. ¿Cómo _____ ellos?

_____.

5. ¿Cómo _____ nosotras?

_____.

6. ¿Cómo _____ yo?

_____.

Realidades A/B

Nombre _____

Hora _____

Capítulo 3B

Fecha _____

Practice Workbook **3B–7**

La buena salud

Your cousin Eva has started a new diet and exercise program, and she has sent you an e-mail telling you all about it. Read her e-mail and answer the questions below in complete sentences.

Hola,

Para mantener la salud, como muchas verduras y frutas cada día. ¡Creo que son sabrosas! Yo hago ejercicio también. Me gusta caminar, pero prefiero levantar pesas. Siempre bebo mucha agua, y es mi bebida favorita. No debemos comer los pasteles, porque son malos para la salud. ¿Estás de acuerdo?

1. ¿Qué come Eva para mantener la salud?

_____

2. ¿Eva hace ejercicio?

_____

3. ¿A Eva le gustan las frutas?

_____

4. ¿Qué prefiere hacer Eva para mantener la salud?

_____

5. ¿Cuál es la bebida favorita de Eva?

_____

6. ¿Por qué no debemos comer los pasteles?

_____

Go Online WEB CODE jcd-0315
PHSchool.com

Realidades A/B

Capítulo 3B

Nombre _____

Fecha _____

Hora _____

Practice Workbook **3B–8**

Repaso

Across

3. el ___

5.

6. Prefiero las ensaladas de ___ y tomate.

8. el ___

10. Debes comer bien para mantener la ___.

12. *drinks*

13. el ___

16. *something*

18. Tengo ___. Necesito comer.

20. estoy de ___

22. Los ___ no son buenos para la salud pero son sabrosos.

24. ___ comer bien para mantener la salud.

Down

1. *meat*

2. un ___

4. las ___ verdes

7. los ___

9. Yo prefiero ___ la salud y comer bien.

11. las ___

14. *carrots*

15. Me gusta la comida de tu mamá. Es muy ___.

17.

19.

21. *dinner*

23. ___ los días; siempre

Organizer

I. Vocabulary

Fruits and vegetables

_____

_____

_____

_____

Starches

_____

_____

_____

_____

General food terms

_____

_____

_____

_____

Types of exercise

_____

_____

_____

_____

II. Grammar

1. Adjectives are _____ when describing one person or thing, and

   _____ when describing more than one person or thing.

2. To make an adjective plural, add _____ if the last letter is a vowel

   and _____ if the last letter is a consonant.

3. The forms of **ser** are: _____ _____

   _____ _____

   _____ _____

Go Online WEB CODE jcd-0316
PHSchool.com

Realidades A/B

Capítulo 4A

Nombre _____

Hora _____

Fecha _____

Practice Workbook **4A–1**

¿Qué hacen?

What do the people in your neighborhood like to do in their free time? Complete the following sentences based on the pictures.

1.  La Sra. García lee un libro en

_____.

2.  Jesús levanta pesas en

_____.

3.  Los lunes tengo _____

con el Sr. Casals.

4.  A Pedro le gusta pasar tiempo en _____

cuando tiene tiempo libre.

5.  Elena y Tomás prefieren ir al _____

los viernes.

6.  A mí me gusta ir a _____

cuando hace calor.

7.  A Sara le gusta caminar en

_____.

8.  Me gusta ir al _____

para comer.

Realidades A/B

Capítulo 4A

Nombre _____

Fecha _____

Hora _____

Practice Workbook **4A–2**

¿Adónde vas?

Where do you go to do the following things? Write your answers in complete sentences. Follow the model.

Modelo	esquiar	*Voy a las montañas para esquiar.*

1. trabajar _____

2. leer, estudiar _____

3. hablar español _____

4. correr, caminar _____

5. ir de compras _____

6. tocar el piano _____

7. comer, beber _____

8. ver una película _____

9. nadar _____

10. hacer ejercicio _____

11. estar con amigos _____

12. levantar pesas _____

Go Online WEB CODE jcd-0401
PHSchool.com

Realidades A/B

Capítulo 4A

Nombre _____

Fecha _____

Hora _____

Practice Workbook **4A–3**

¿Qué hacen?

An exchange student from Chile wants to know where people go to do certain activities. Complete each conversation with the verb suggested by the first picture, then answer the questions based on the second illustration.

Modelo

—Cuando __*ves*__ una película, ¿adónde vas?

—__*Voy al cine*__.

1.

—Cuando _____, ¿adónde vas?

—_____.

2.

—Cuando _____, ¿adónde vas?

—_____.

3.

—Cuando _____, ¿adónde vas?

—_____.

4.

—Cuando _____, ¿adónde vas?

—_____.

5.

—Cuando _____, ¿adónde vas?

—_____.

6.

—Cuando _____, ¿adónde vas?

—_____.

Realidades A/B

Capítulo 4A

Nombre _____

Hora _____

Fecha _____

Practice Workbook **4A–4**

El horario de Tito

Look at Tito's schedule for part of the month of February. Then answer the questions about his activities in complete sentences.

F E B R E R O						
lunes	*martes*	*miércoles*	*jueves*	*viernes*	*sábado*	*domingo*
8 trabajar	**9** nadar	**10** estudiar en la biblioteca	**11** trabajar	**12** ir al cine	**13** ir al gimnasio	**14** ir a la iglesia
15 trabajar	**16** practicar karate	**17** estudiar en la biblioteca	**18** trabajar	**19** ir al cine	**20** ir al gimnasio	**21** ir a la iglesia
22 trabajar	**23** levantar pesas	**24** estudiar en la biblioteca	**25** trabajar	**26** ir al cine	**27** ir al gimnasio	**28** ir a la iglesia

1. ¿Qué hace Tito los viernes?

   _____

2. ¿Cuándo estudia Tito en la biblioteca?

   _____

3. ¿Cuándo hace ejercicio Tito?

   _____

4. Generalmente, ¿cuándo trabaja Tito?

   _____

5. ¿Qué hace Tito los lunes?

   _____

6. ¿Cuándo va a la iglesia Tito?

   _____

7. ¿Qué hace Tito los fines de semana?

   _____

Go Online WEB CODE jcd-0402
PHSchool.com

Las actividades favoritas

Students are making plans for what they will do after school. Complete their conversations with the correct forms of the verb **ir**.

1. LOLIS: Hoy, (yo) _____ al parque después de las clases.

ELIA: ¡Qué bien! María y yo _____ al cine.

LOLIS: Mi amigo Pablo también _____ al cine hoy.

2. MARTA: Hola, Juan. ¿Adónde _____?

JUAN: Pues, _____ a la clase de inglés, pero después

_____ al centro comercial. ¿Y tú?

MARTA: Pues, mis padres _____ a la playa y yo

_____ con ellos.

JUAN: ¡Qué bueno! ¿Cuándo _____ Uds.?

MARTA: Nosotros _____ después de las clases.

3. RODOLFO: ¡Hola, Pablo, Felipe!

PABLO Y FELIPE: ¡Hola, Rodolfo!

RODOLFO: ¿Adónde _____ Uds.?

PABLO: Pues, yo _____ a casa con unos amigos.

FELIPE: Yo no _____ con él. _____ a la mezquita.

¿Y tú?

RODOLFO: Catrina y yo _____ a la piscina. Ella _____

al gimnasio más tarde.

PABLO: Mi amiga Elena _____ al gimnasio con ella. Creo que

ellas _____ a las cinco.

FELIPE: Es muy tarde. Tengo que _____. ¡Hasta luego!

Realidades A/B

Capítulo 4A

Nombre _____

Hora _____

Fecha _____

Practice Workbook **4A–6**

La pregunta perfecta

A. Complete the following questions with the correct question words.

1. ¿_____ es el chico más alto de la clase?

2. ¿_____ vas al cine? ¿Hoy?

3. ¿_____ es tu número de teléfono?

4. ¿_____ te llamas?

5. ¿_____ vas después de las clases hoy?

6. ¿_____ está mi libro de español?

7. ¿_____ es esto?

8. ¿_____ años tienes?

B. Now, form your own questions using some of the question words above.

1. ¿_____?

2. ¿_____?

3. ¿_____?

4. ¿_____?

5. ¿_____?

6. ¿_____?

7. ¿_____?

Realidades A/B

Capítulo 4A

Nombre _____

Hora _____

Fecha _____

Practice Workbook **4A–7**

¿Qué haces?

You are talking with your parents about your plans for the evening. They have lots of questions. Your answers are given below. Write your parents' questions in the spaces provided.

TUS PADRES: ¿_____?

TÚ: Voy a un restaurante.

TUS PADRES: ¿_____?

TÚ: Voy con unos amigos.

TUS PADRES: ¿_____?

TÚ: Ellos se llaman Roberto y Ana.

TUS PADRES: ¿_____?

TÚ: Roberto y Ana son de México.

TUS PADRES: ¿_____?

TÚ: Pues, Roberto es inteligente, trabajador y paciente.

TUS PADRES: ¿_____?

TÚ: Ana es deportista y estudiosa.

TUS PADRES: ¿_____?

TÚ: Después, nosotros vamos al cine.

TUS PADRES: ¿_____?

TÚ: ¿Después? Pues, voy a casa. ¡Uds. hacen muchas preguntas!

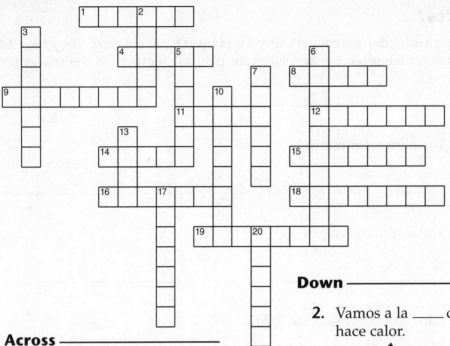

Realidades A/B

Capítulo 4A

Nombre _____

Fecha _____

Hora _____

Practice Workbook **4A–8**

Repaso

Down

2. Vamos a la _____ cuando hace calor.

3.

5. Me gusta caminar en el _____.

6.

7. el _____ comercial

10. Voy al _____ para levantar pesas.

13. Vamos al _____ para ver una película.

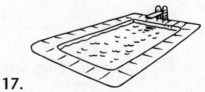

17.

20. Vas al _____ para trabajar.

Across

1. *temple*

4.

8. ¡No me _____!

9. *mosque*

11. –¿Con _____ vas al cine?
– Con Ana.

12. Tengo que ir a la _____ de piano.

14. No tengo tiempo _____.

15. Para la Navidad todos van de _____.

16. *after*

18. Me gusta la _____ *Desperado*.

19.

Realidades A/B

Capítulo 4A

Nombre _____

Fecha _____

Hora _____

Practice Workbook **4A–9**

Organizer

I. Vocabulary

Some of my favorite places

_____
_____
_____
_____
_____
_____

Words to talk about other places

_____
_____
_____
_____
_____
_____

Interrogative words

_____
_____
_____
_____
_____
_____
_____
_____

Phrases related to leisure activities

_____
_____
_____
_____
_____
_____
_____
_____

II. Grammar

1. The forms of the verb **ir** are: _____ _____

   _____ _____

   _____ _____

2. **A.** In order to get information in English, we use the words *who, what, where, when, why,* and *how*. In Spanish these words are: _____, _____,

   _____, _____, _____ y _____.

   B. When asking a question in Spanish, the verb comes _____ the subject.

Realidades A/B

Capítulo 4B

Nombre _____

Fecha _____

Hora _____

Practice Workbook **4B–1**

¿Eres deportista?

Write the name of the sport or activity indicated by the art.

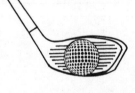

1. _____

2. _____

3. _____

4. _____

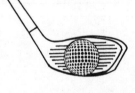

5. _____

6. _____

7. _____

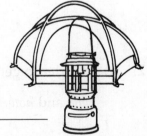

8. _____

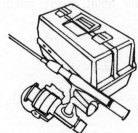

9. _____

Go Online WEB CODE jcd-0411
PHSchool.com

Realidades A/B

Capítulo 4B

Nombre _____

Fecha _____

Hora _____

Practice Workbook **4B–2**

Las invitaciones

You and your friends are making plans for the weekend. Complete your friends' invitations with the activities suggested by the pictures. Then accept the offers using complete sentences. Follow the model.

Modelo

—¿Te gustaría _____*ir al cine*_____ este fin de semana?

—_____*Sí, me gustaría ir al cine*_____.

1.

—¿Puedes _____ este fin de semana?

—_____.

2.

—¿Quieres _____ este fin de semana?

—_____.

3.

—¿Puedes _____ este fin de semana?

—_____.

4.

—¿Te gustaría _____ este fin de semana?

—_____.

5.

—¿Quieres _____ este fin de semana?

—_____.

Realidades A/B

Capítulo 4B

Nombre _____

Fecha _____

Hora _____

Practice Workbook **4B–3**

¿Cómo están?

You have just arrived at school and are asking how your friends are doing. Using the pictures to help you, fill in the blanks with the correct form of **estar** and the appropriate adjective. Don't forget to make the adjective agree with the subject!

—¿Cómo está ella?

1. —_____.

—¿Cómo está él?

2. —_____.

—¿Cómo están ellos?

3. —_____.

—¿Cómo están ellas?

4. —_____.

—¿Cómo están los estudiantes?

5. —_____.

—¿Cómo está él?

6. —_____.

Go Online   WEB CODE jcd-0412
PHSchool.com

¿A qué hora?

Lucía is very busy on the weekends. Answer the questions about her schedule using complete sentences.

Modelo   ¿A qué hora usa la computadora?

Usa la computadora a las siete y media de la noche.

1. ¿A qué hora tiene que trabajar Lucía?

_____

2. ¿A qué hora va a casa?

_____

3. ¿Qué hacen Lucía y su amiga a las ocho de la mañana?

_____

4. ¿A qué hora come la cena Lucía?

_____

5. ¿Cuándo estudian ella y su amigo?

_____

6. ¿Adónde va Lucía esta noche? ¿A qué hora?

_____

Realidades A/B

Capítulo 4B

Nombre _____

Hora _____

Fecha _____

Practice Workbook **4B–5**

Los planes

It is 10:00 Saturday morning, and you and your friends are making plans for the afternoon and evening. Using a form of **ir** + **a** + *infinitive*, write complete sentences about everyone's plans. Follow the model.

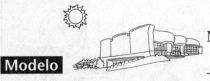 María

Modelo *María va a ir de compras esta tarde* .

 Ana y yo

1. _____ .

Pablo

2. _____ .

Yo

3. _____ .

 Mis amigos

4. _____ .

 Tú

5. _____ .

Nosotros

6. _____ .

 Ud.

7. _____ .

 Ana y Lorena

8. _____ .

Go Online WEB CODE jcd-0413
PHSchool.com

Realidades A/B

Capítulo 4B

Nombre _____

Hora _____

Fecha _____

Practice Workbook **4B–6**

Demasiadas preguntas

Your friends are asking you to make plans for this weekend, but you are not able to do anything that they have suggested. Using the pictures to help you, respond to their questions using **ir** + **a** + *infinitive.* Follow the model.

¿Puedes ir al partido mañana?

Modelo   *No, no puedo. Voy a correr mañana*

¿Quieres ir al partido esta noche?

1. _____.

¿Te gustaría ir al cine conmigo esta noche?

2. _____.

¿Quieres jugar al golf esta tarde?

3. _____.

¿Puedes jugar videojuegos conmigo el viernes?

4. _____.

¿Te gustaría ir de compras mañana por la noche?

5. _____.

¿Te gustaría ir al baile conmigo esta noche?

6. _____.

¿Quieres ir a la biblioteca conmigo?

7. _____.

¿Puedes ir de cámping conmigo este fin de semana?

8. _____.

Realidades **A/B**

Capítulo 4B

Nombre _____

Hora _____

Fecha _____

Practice Workbook **4B–7**

¿A qué juegas?

Friends are talking about the sports that they enjoy playing. Write the correct form of the verb **jugar** to complete each sentence.

1. —¿Marta juega al vóleibol?

    —Sí, Rodrigo y ella _____ todos los días.

2. —Oye, ¿puedes jugar al básquetbol con nosotros?

    —Lo siento, pero no _____ bien.

3. —¿A qué juegan Uds.?

    —Nosotros _____ al golf.

4. —Ellas juegan al tenis muy bien, ¿no?

    —Sí, _____ muy bien.

5. —¿_____ Ud. al básquetbol a la una?

    —No. Tengo que ir a un concierto.

6. —Yo juego al fútbol hoy.

    —¡Ay, me encanta el fútbol! ¡_____ contigo!

7. —¿Tú y Manuel jugáis al béisbol esta tarde?

    —Sí. ¡_____ todos los días!

8. —¿Qué hace Luz esta noche?

    —Ella _____ al vóleibol a las ocho.

Realidades A/B

Capítulo 4B

Nombre _____

Hora _____

Fecha _____

Practice Workbook **4B-8**

Repaso

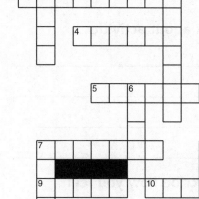

Across

3. No puedo jugar. Estoy ____ ocupado.

4. *sad*

5.

7. Me gusta ver el ____ de béisbol.

9. yo sé, tú ____

10. Lo ____, pero no puedo.

12.  el fútbol ____

15.

17. El *Jitterbug* es un ____.

19. *Great!*

20. Vamos al ____ para escuchar música.

21. *with me*

Down

1. Vamos a la ____ de cumpleaños de Paco.

2.

6. *afternoon;* la ____

7. me gusta ir de *fishing*

8. el ____ de semana

11. Ella trabaja mucho, siempre está ____.

13.

14. Es después de la tarde; la ____.

16. *Hey!*

17.

18. Voy a la escuela a las siete de la ____.

Organizer

I. Vocabulary

Words to talk about activities

_____

_____

_____

_____

Words to describe how you feel

_____

_____

_____

_____

Words to accept or decline an invitation

_____

_____

_____

_____

_____

Names of sports

_____

_____

_____

_____

_____

Words to say when something happens

_____

_____

_____

_____

_____

II. Grammar

1. The forms of the verb **jugar** are: _____ _____

   _____ _____

   _____ _____

2. The preposition **con** becomes _____ to mean "with me" and _____ to mean "with you."

3. To say you are going to do something, you use the verb _____ + _____ + the action you are going to perform.

Go Online WEB CODE jcd-0416
PHSchool.com

Realidades A/B

Capítulo 5A

Nombre _____

Fecha _____

Hora _____

Practice Workbook **5A–1**

La familia

A. Patricia is telling you about her family. Label each person in her family tree with a word that describes his or her relationship to Patricia. You may use some words more than once.

Patricia _____ _____ _____ _____   _____ _____ _____

B. Now, answer the following questions by circling **sí** or **no**.

1. ¿Patricia tiene hermanastros?   Sí   No

2. ¿Patricia tiene hermanas mayores?   Sí   No

3. ¿Patricia tiene dieciséis años?   Sí   No

4. ¿Patricia tiene tres primos menores?   Sí   No

5. ¿Patricia tiene dos abuelas?   Sí   No

Realidades A/B

Capítulo 5A

Nombre _____

Hora _____

Fecha _____

Practice Workbook **5A–2**

¿Quién es?

A. Complete the sentences below with the correct family relationships.

1. Mi ___ ___ (___) es la esposa de mi tío.

2. Mis ___ ___ ___ (___) ___ ___ ___ son los hijos de mis padres.

3. Mi ___ ___ (___) ___ ___ es el hijo del hermano de mi padre.

4. Mi (___) ___ ___ ___ ___ ___ es la madre de mi madre.

5. Mi ___ ___ ___ ___ ___ ___ ___ (___) ___ es el esposo de mi madre (no es mi padre).

6. Yo soy la ___ ___ ___ (___) de mis padres.

7. Mi ___ ___ ___ (___) ___ es la hija de la hermana de mi padre.

8. Mis (___) ___ ___ ___ son los hermanos de mis padres.

9. Mamá y papá son mis ___ ___ (___) ___ ___ ___ .

10. Mis ___ ___ (___) ___ ___ ___ ___ (___) ___ ___ ___ ___ son las hijas de la esposa de mi padre (no son mis hermanas).

B. Now, unscramble the circled letters to come up with another member of the family.

___ ___ ___ ___ ___ ___ ___ ___ ___ ___ ___

Go **Online** WEB CODE jcd-0501
PHSchool.com

Realidades A/B

Capítulo 5A

Nombre _____

Hora _____

Fecha _____

Practice Workbook **5A–3**

¡Una fiesta inesperada (*a surprise party*)!

The Rodríguez family is giving their older son Tomás a surprise birthday party. Complete their conversation, using the most logical word from the word bank.

luces	la piñata	tiene	decoraciones
dulces	pastel	celebrar	sólo
globos	sacar fotos	regalos	

MAMÁ: Vamos a hacer el plan porque vamos a _____ el cumpleaños

de Tomás. Él _____ doce años.

TÍA LULÚ: Sí, ¡vamos a celebrar! Primero, necesitamos un _____ para

comer ¿no? ¡Qué sabroso!

MAMÁ: Sí. Y necesitamos unas _____ perfectas. Vamos a necesitar un

globo y una luz.

TÍA LULÚ: ¿_____ *un* globo y *una* luz? ¡No, necesitamos muchos

_____ y muchas _____! También

necesitamos papel picado.

PABLITO: Oye, ¡yo tengo una cámara fabulosa! Puedo _____ en la fiesta

cuando Tomás abre los _____ .

MAMÁ: Sí, Pablito. ¡Muchas gracias! Y finalmente, pueden romper

_____ . ¿Tenemos _____?

TÍA LULÚ: Sí, tenemos muchos dulces.

PABLITO: ¡Qué buena fiesta!

Realidades A/B

Capítulo 5A

Nombre _____

Fecha _____

Hora _____

Practice Workbook **5A–4**

La celebración

Raúl is explaining how he and his family are preparing for his sister's birthday party. Read his description and answer the questions that follow in complete sentences.

> Hoy es el cumpleaños de mi hermana menor, Gabriela. Mis padres y yo preparamos la fiesta. Mi mamá decora con el papel picado y las luces. Mi papá tiene los regalos y los globos. Yo preparo la mesa con los globos y el pastel. También tengo la cámara porque voy a hacer un video de la fiesta.
>
> Sólo nuestra familia va a estar aquí, pero con todos mis primos, mis tíos y mis abuelos tenemos muchas personas. A las cinco mi hermana va a estar aquí y la fiesta va a empezar.

1. ¿Quién es Gabriela? _____

2. ¿Para quién es la fiesta? _____

3. ¿Qué clase de fiesta es? _____

4. ¿Con qué decora Raúl? _____

5. ¿Qué tiene el papá? _____

6. ¿Qué va a hacer Raúl? _____

7. ¿Quiénes van a estar en la fiesta? _____

_____

8. ¿A qué hora va a empezar la fiesta? _____

Go Online WEB CODE jcd-0502
PHSchool.com

Realidades A/B

Capítulo 5A

Nombre _____

Hora _____

Fecha _____

Practice Workbook **5A–5**

Conversaciones

You overhear a group of students talking. Fill in the blanks in their conversations with the correct forms of the verb **tener**.

1. FRANCO: Hola, Carmen. ¿Qué tienes en la mano?

CARMEN: (Yo) _____ un regalo para mi primo. Es su cumpleaños.

FRANCO: Ah, ¿sí? ¿Cuántos años _____?

CARMEN: _____ doce años.

FRANCO: Mis primos también _____ doce años.

2. ELENA: ¡Oye, Carlos! ¿Cuántos años _____?

CARLOS: ¿Yo? Yo _____ quince años. ¿Por qué?

ELENA: Porque mi hermano y yo _____ una prima de quince

años que _____ que ir a un baile el viernes. ¿(Tú)

_____ planes?

CARLOS: ¿El viernes? No, no _____ otros planes.

3. PABLO: Hola, José. Hola, Manolo. ¿(Uds.) _____ un dólar?

JOSÉ: Sí, yo _____ un dólar. ¿Por qué?

PABLO: Porque yo _____ hambre y quiero comprar un perrito

caliente.

MANOLO: ¿La cafetería _____ perritos calientes buenos?

PABLO: Sí. ¿Quieres uno?

JOSÉ: Sí, pero primero Manolo y yo _____ que ir a clase.

PABLO: También _____ que ir a clase.

Realidades A/B

Capítulo 5A

Nombre _____

Hora _____

Fecha _____

Practice Workbook **5A–6**

¿De quién es?

A. Fill in the following chart with the masculine and feminine, singular and plural forms of the possessive adjectives indicated.

hijo	tía	abuelos	hermanas
			mis hermanas
	tu tía		
su hijo			
		nuestros abuelos	
vuestro hijo	*vuestra tía*	*vuestros abuelos*	*vuestras hermanas*

B. Now, complete the following sentences by writing in the possessive adjective that corresponds with the English adjective in parentheses. Follow the model.

Modelo (*my*) _____Mi_____ abuela es vieja.

1. (*our*) _____ abuelos van a la casa para hablar con nosotros.

2. (*your*) Sara, gracias por _____ libro.

3. (*my*) _____ prima es de Tejas.

4. (*your*) ¿Tienen mucha tarea en _____ clase de matemáticas?

5. (*their*) _____ tíos están en la oficina ahora.

6. (*my*) El perro come _____ galletas.

7. (*our*) Nosotros vamos a la escuela en _____ bicicletas.

8. (*your*) Profesor, ¿dónde está _____ oficina?

9. (*their*) _____ hijo es muy trabajador.

10. (*his*) _____ hermana está enferma.

Go Online WEB CODE jcd-0505
PHSchool.com

Realidades A/B

Capítulo 5A

Nombre _____

Hora _____

Fecha _____

Practice Workbook **5A–7**

Los regalos perfectos

Using the subjects below and the activities suggested by the pictures, write complete sentences about what your friends and relatives have for the party. Make sure you use the correct possessive adjective. Follow the model.

Mi primo Juan

Modelo *Mi primo Juan tiene su cámara.* _____

Mis tíos

1. _____

Alicia

2. _____

Tú

3. _____

Nosotros

4. _____

Yo

5. _____

Ud.

6. _____

La profesora Méndez

7. _____

Nosotras

8. _____

Realidades Ⓐ/Ⓑ

Capítulo 5A

Nombre _____

Fecha _____

Hora _____

Practice Workbook **5A–8**

Repaso

Across

5. La madre de mi primo es mi ____.

7. El hermano de mi padre es mi ____.

9. *sister*

11.

13. mi papá; el ____

16. La mamá de mi padre es mi ____.

17. Mi hermano y yo somos los ____ de nuestros padres.

19.

20.

21. mi mamá; la ____

Down

1. El esposo de mi madre; no es mi papá, es mi ____.

2. *brother*

3.

4. el papel ____

6.

8. ¡Feliz ____! ¿Cuántos años tienes?

9. Quiero ____ un video.

10. la madre de mi hermanastro; mi ____

12. Los hijos ____ la piñata.

14. Es el hermano de mi prima; mi ____.

15. ¿Quién ____ las fotos de la fiesta?

18. *parents*

21. no menor

Realidades **A/B**

Capítulo 5A

Nombre _____

Hora _____

Fecha _____

Practice Workbook **5A-9**

Organizer

I. Vocabulary

To describe family relationships

_____

_____

_____

_____

_____

_____

_____

_____

Activities at a party

_____

_____

_____

_____

Items at a party

_____

_____

_____

_____

_____

Words to express possession

_____

_____

_____

_____

_____

II. Grammar

1. The forms of **tener** are: _____ _____

_____ _____

_____ _____

2. Possessive adjectives in Spanish are written as follows:

	Singular/Plural		Singular/Plural
my	_____ / _____	our	_____ / _____
your (familiar)	_____ / _____	your (pl., familiar)	_____ / _____
your (formal), his, hers	_____ / _____	your (pl., formal), their	_____ / _____

Nombre _____   Hora _____

Fecha _____   Practice Workbook **5B–1**

Restaurante elegante

Label the following items with the correct word. Don't forget to use the correct definite article (**el** or **la**).

1. _____   5. _____   9. _____

2. _____   6. _____   10. _____

3. _____   7. _____   11. _____

4. _____   8. _____

Go Online WEB CODE jcd-0511
PHSchool.com

Las descripciones

You are telling your friends about some of your family members. Write descriptions of them in complete sentences. Follow the model.

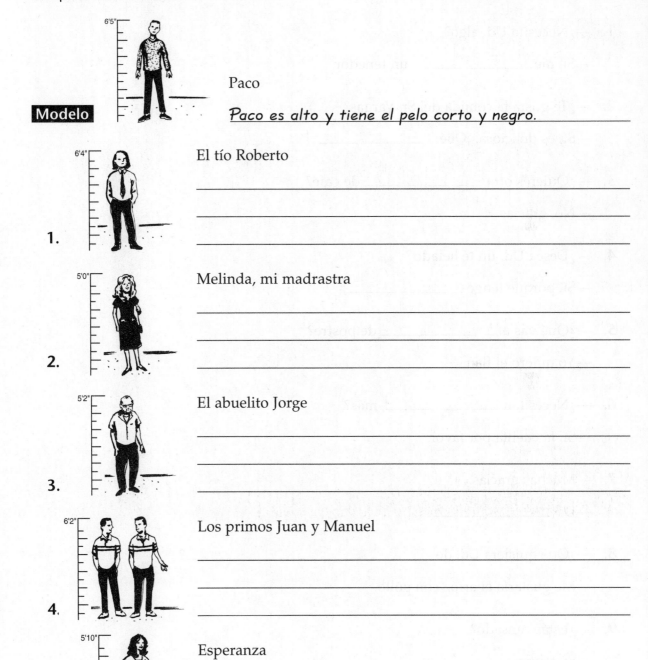

Paco

Modelo *Paco es alto y tiene el pelo corto y negro.*

El tío Roberto

1. _____

_____

_____

Melinda, mi madrastra

2. _____

_____

_____

El abuelito Jorge

3. _____

_____

_____

Los primos Juan y Manuel

4. _____

_____

_____

Esperanza

5. _____

_____

_____

La palabra correcta

Complete the following mini-conversations with the most logical words or phrases from your vocabulary.

1. —¿Necesita Ud. algo?

—Sí, me _____ un tenedor.

2. —¿Te gusta la comida del Sr. Vargas?

—Sí, es deliciosa. ¡Qué _____!

3. —¿Quieres otra _____ de café?

—No, gracias.

4. —¿Desea Ud. un té helado?

—Sí, porque tengo _____.

5. —¿Qué vas a _____ de postre?

—Yo quiero el flan.

6. —¿Necesitan _____ más?

—Sí, la cuenta por favor.

7. —Muchas gracias.

—De _____.

8. —¿Qué quisiera Ud. de _____ _____?

—Me gustaría el arroz con pollo.

9. —¿Estás cansado?

—Sí, tengo _____.

10. —¿Bebes el café?

—Sí, porque tengo _____.

Realidades A/B

Capítulo 5B

Nombre _____

Hora _____

Fecha _____

Practice Workbook **5B–4**

Cita (*date*) en español

A. David and Rocío are on a date at a Spanish restaurant. Using the vocabulary you have learned in this chapter, write their possible responses to the waiter's questions. Use complete sentences.

CAMARERO: ¿Qué desean Uds. de plato principal?

DAVID: _____

ROCÍO: _____

CAMARERO: ¿Cómo está la comida?

DAVID: _____

ROCÍO: _____

CAMARERO: ¿Desean algo más?

DAVID: _____

ROCÍO: _____

B. Now, based on the waiter's responses, write what you think David or Rocío may have asked the waiter.

DAVID: ¿_____?

CAMARERO: Sí, le traigo una servilleta.

ROCÍO: ¿_____?

CAMARERO: Sí, ahora puede pedir algo de postre.

DAVID: ¿_____?

CAMARERO: Un café, por supuesto. ¿Tiene sueño?

Go Online
PHSchool.com WEB CODE jcd-0512

Realidades A/B

Capítulo 5B

Nombre _____

Hora _____

Fecha _____

Practice Workbook **5B–5**

¿Quién viene?

Your class has decided to put on a talent show, and you are in charge of scheduling what time everyone is coming to audition for different skits. Your friend Lola is anxious to know the schedule. Answer her questions using the picture below. Follow the model.

Modelo ¿Quién viene a las ocho y media?

La Sra. Ramos viene a las ocho y media.

1. ¿Quién viene a las nueve?

_____

2. ¿Quién viene a las diez?

_____

3. ¿Quién viene a las once menos cuarto?

_____

4. ¿Quién viene a las once y media?

_____

5. ¿Quién viene a las doce?

_____

6. ¿Quién viene a la una?

_____

7. ¿Quién viene a las dos y media?

_____

8. ¿Quién viene a las tres y media?

_____

Go Online WEB CODE jcd-0513
PHSchool.com

Una carta para mamá

Read the following letter from Rosaura to her mom in Spain. Write the form of **ser** or **estar** that best completes each sentence.

Querida mamá:

¡Aquí _____ en Chicago! Chicago _____ una gran ciudad

con muchas personas que _____ muy interesantes. La comida

_____ fantástica. La especialidad _____ la pizza. ¡Qué rica!

Vivo con una familia muy simpática. Tienen un hijo que siempre

_____ contento y una hija que _____ muy estudiosa.

¡_____ las nueve de la noche y ella _____ en la biblioteca!

Los chicos de la escuela también _____ estudiosos, pero no muy

serios. Mis compañeros y yo _____ muy buenos amigos y

_____ juntos todos los fines de semana. Una amiga, Vera,

_____ boliviana y _____ divertidísima. Vera y yo

_____ en la misma clase de biología.

Bueno, mamá, _____ muy tarde. Mañana voy a _____

muy ocupada y necesito dormir. Pero sabes ahora que todo _____

bien aquí y que yo _____ contenta. Besos para ti y para papá.

Un abrazo,

Rosaura

Realidades **A/B**

Capítulo 5B

Nombre _____

Hora _____

Fecha _____

Practice Workbook **5B–7**

¿Qué van a comer?

The Vázquez family is getting ready to order dinner in a restaurant. Look at the pictures to get an idea of the person's needs. Answer the questions below using vocabulary that would most logically go in each situation.

1.

¿Cómo está la Sra. Vázquez? _____

¿Qué debe pedir de plato principal? _____

¿De postre? _____ ¿Y para beber? _____

2.

¿Cómo están los chicos? _____

¿Qué deben pedir de plato principal? _____

¿De postre? _____ ¿Y para beber? _____

3.

¿Cómo está Elisita? _____

¿Qué debe pedir de plato principal? _____

¿De postre? _____ ¿Y para beber? _____

4.

¿Cómo está el Sr. Vázquez? _____

¿Qué debe pedir de plato principal? _____

¿De postre? _____ ¿Y para beber? _____

Go Online WEB CODE jcd-0515 PHSchool.com

Realidades A/B

Capítulo 5B

Nombre _____

Fecha _____

Hora _____

Practice Workbook **5B–8**

Repaso

Across

6. *blond;* el pelo ____

7. No bajo ____.

8. Uds. ____ cansados.

12. Paquito no es viejo. Es ____.

13. ¡Camarero, la ____ por favor!

15.

16. Mi abuela tiene el pelo ____.

17. Ella tiene 88 años. Es ____.

18. Necesito un cuchillo y un ____ para comer el bistec.

19. sal y ____

21. Necesito un té. Tengo ____.

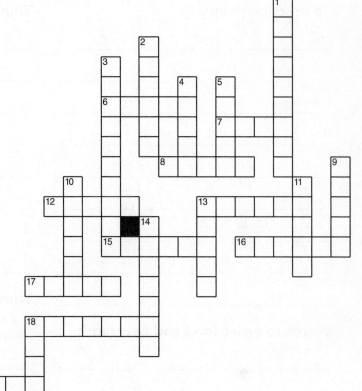

Down

1. *red-haired (m.)*

2. El Sr. López es un ____.

3. *napkin*

4. Nosotros ____ bajos.

5. *good-looking (f.)*

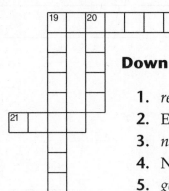

9. ____ el pelo ____

10. ¿Qué quieres de ____? El flan.

11. Quiero un té helado. Tengo ____.

13. no largo

14.

18. Quiero una ____ de café.

19. el plato ____

20. La Sra. Miranda es una ____.

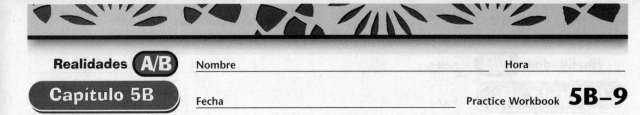

Organizer

I. Vocabulary

To describe people

_____

_____

_____

_____

_____

_____

_____

_____

Words to order food and beverages

_____

_____

_____

_____

Things at a restaurant

_____

_____

_____

_____

_____

_____

_____

Words to describe how you're feeling

_____

_____

_____

_____

II. Grammar

1. The forms of **venir** are: _____ _____

_____ _____

_____ _____

2. For physical and personality descriptions, and to tell what time it is, use the verb

_____. To talk about location and physical and emotional states,

use the verb _____.

Go Online WEB CODE jcd-0516
PHSchool.com

Un dormitorio nuevo para mí

Ignacio is moving into his sister's room when she goes away to college. His parents have told him that he can bring anything into his new room that he can carry by himself. Make a list of eight things that he would definitely be able to bring with him, and five things that he definitely wouldn't be able to bring. Use the examples given to help you.

Traer conmigo

　　　　　　　　　　　　El lector DVD
_____
_____
_____
_____
_____
_____
_____

No traer conmigo

　　　　　　　　　　　　La pared
_____
_____
_____
_____
_____

Realidades **A/B**

Capítulo 6A

Nombre _____

Hora _____

Fecha _____

Practice Workbook **6A–2**

Muchos colores

Write the names of the color or colors that you associate with the following things. Don't forget to make the colors agree in gender and number.

1. el jugo de naranja _____.

2. la limonada _____.

3. el 14 de febrero _____.

4. el 25 de diciembre _____.

5. el sol _____.

6. la nieve _____.

7. unas zanahorias _____.

8. la bandera de los Estados Unidos _____.

9. un tomate _____.

10. la piscina _____.

11. la noche _____.

12. el Día de San Patricio _____.

Go Online WEB CODE jcd-0601
PHSchool.com

La experiencia nueva

A. Read the letter that Gloria wrote to her friend in Spain about her host family in Chile.

Querida Sandra,

Lo paso muy bien aquí con la familia Quijano. Desde el primer día aquí, tengo mi propio dormitorio. Hay una cama, una mesita, una lámpara, un escritorio con una silla pequeña y un espejo. También hay una ventana con cortinas amarillas. La mejor cosa del cuarto es la lámpara. Es roja, negra y marrón y es muy artística. Creo que es la lámpara más bonita del mundo.

El cuarto también es bonito. Las paredes son moradas. Sólo quiero mi equipo de sonido y mis discos compactos.

Abrazos,

Gloria

B. Now, answer these questions in complete sentences.

1. ¿A Gloria le gusta la familia?

_____

2. ¿Comparte Gloria el dormitorio con otro estudiante?

_____

3. ¿De qué color son las paredes en el dormitorio de Gloria?

_____

4. ¿Tiene Gloria su equipo de sonido en su dormitorio?

_____

5. ¿Cómo es la lámpara en el dormitorio de Gloria? ¿A ella le gusta?

_____

6. ¿De qué color son las cortinas en el dormitorio de Gloria?

_____

Realidades A/B

Capítulo 6A

Nombre _____

Hora _____

Fecha _____

Practice Workbook **6A–4**

¿Dónde está todo?

Movers just finished putting everything into Marcela's new room. Help her locate everything by describing where the items are in the picture below. Follow the model.

Modelo *Una lámpara está al lado del televisor.*

_____

_____

_____

_____

_____

_____

_____

Go Online WEB CODE jcd-0602
PHSchool.com

Las comparaciones

Felipe and Mónica are brother and sister who are very different from each other. Using their pictures and the model to help you, write comparisons of the two siblings. Remember to make the adjectives agree in gender with the subject.

Modelo   Mónica / alto   *Mónica es más alta que Felipe.* _____

1. Felipe / serio _____

2. Mónica / sociable _____

3. Mónica / rubio _____

4. Felipe / estudioso _____

5. Felipe / alto _____

6. Mónica / viejo _____

7. Felipe / rubio _____

8. Felipe / joven _____

9. Mónica / serio _____

Realidades A/B

Capítulo 6A

Nombre _____

Fecha _____

Hora _____

Practice Workbook **6A–6**

Los premios Óscar

The following chart rates movies according to certain categories. Four stars is the best rating, one star is the worst rating. Using the chart as a guide, write complete sentences comparing the three movies. Follow the model.

	Una tarde en agosto	*Mi vida*	*Siete meses en Lima*
Actores – talentosos	****	**	***
Fotografía – artística	****	*	***
Ropa – bonita	***	****	***
Director – creativo	****	***	**
Cuento – interesante	****	**	*

Modelo   actores / "Una tarde en agosto"

Los actores de "Una tarde en agosto" son los más talentosos.

1. fotografía / "Una tarde en agosto"

   _____

2. fotografía / "Mi vida"

   _____

3. director / "Una tarde en agosto"

   _____

4. actores / "Una tarde en agosto"

   _____

5. director / "Siete meses en Lima"

   _____

6. ropa / "Mi vida"

   _____

7. cuento / "Siete meses en Lima"

   _____

8. actores / "Mi vida"

   _____

9. cuento / "Una tarde en agosto"

   _____

Go Online WEB CODE jcd-0604
PHSchool.com

Realidades A/B

Capítulo 6A

Nombre _____

Fecha _____

Hora _____

Practice Workbook **6A–7**

Las mini-conversaciones

A. Fill in the rest of these conjugations.

	DORMIR	**PODER**
yo		
tú		*puedes*
él, ella, Ud.	*duerme*	
nosotros		
vosotros	*dormís*	*podéis*
ellos, ellas, Uds.		

B. Write the correct forms of either **dormir** or **poder** in the blanks to complete the mini-conversations below.

1. —¿Quieres ir al cine?

   —No _____ . Tengo que trabajar.

2. —¿Cuántas horas _____ cada noche?

   —Generalmente ocho horas.

3. —¿Uds. _____ venir a nuestra fiesta?

   —Sí. ¿A qué hora es?

4. —Nosotros no _____ trabajar hoy.

   —Está bien. Van a trabajar mañana.

5. —Cuando ellas van de cámping, ¿dónde _____ ?

   —Pues, en sus camas Coleman, por supuesto.

6. —¿Qué haces a las once y media de la noche?

   —¡Yo _____ !

7. —¿_____ (tú) hablar con tu abuela por teléfono?

   —No, no _____ porque estoy ocupado.

8. —¿Qué hace una chica cansada?

   —_____ mucho.

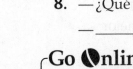
WEB CODE jcd-0605
PHSchool.com

Realidades A/B

Capítulo 6A

Nombre _____

Hora _____

Fecha _____

Practice Workbook **6A–8**

Repaso

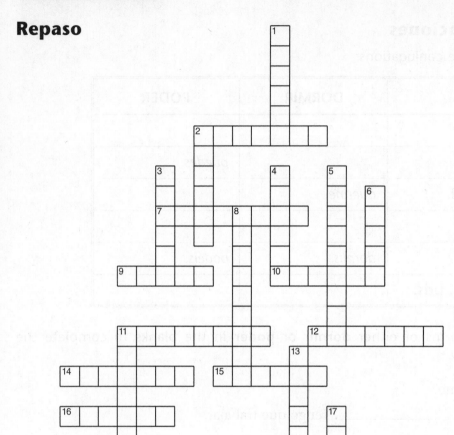

© Pearson Education, Inc. All rights reserved.

Down

1. Tengo que ___ por la noche.

2.

3. el ___ DVD

4. no pequeño

5.

6. un ___ compacto

8. no es a la derecha; es a la ___

11. Un plátano es de color ___.

13. *dresser*

17. La nieve es de color ___.

18. no mejor

Across

2. Rojo y azul son ___.

7.

9.

10. el ___ de sonido

11. Hay una ___ debajo de la cama.

12. Uds. tienen mucha ropa en el ___.

14. Los libros están en el ___.

15. *brown*

16. no es fea, es ___

19. Duermo en la ___.

20. *mirror*

Organizer

I. Vocabulary

To talk about things in a bedroom

_____
_____
_____
_____
_____

Words to describe things

_____
_____
_____
_____

Electronic equipment

_____
_____
_____
_____

Words to talk about colors

_____
_____
_____

II. Grammar

1. To compare peoples' ages, use either _____ + **que** or _____ + **que**. To say that something is "better than" use _____ + **que**; to say that something is "worse than" use _____ + **que**.

2. To say that something is the "best" or "worst" use the following construction: article + _____ / _____ + noun. To say "most" or "least" the construction is article + noun + _____ / _____ + adjective.

3. The forms of **poder** are:

_____ _____
_____ _____
_____ _____

The forms of **dormir** are:

_____ _____
_____ _____
_____ _____

Realidades A/B

Capítulo 6B

Nombre _____

Fecha _____

Hora _____

Practice Workbook **6B–1**

Los cuartos

The Suárez family has just moved into a new house. Tell what rooms are on each floor of the house.

En la planta baja hay: _____

_____

_____

En el primer piso hay: _____

_____

_____

_____

_____

Go Online
PHSchool.com WEB CODE jcd-0611

Realidades A/B

Capítulo 6B

Nombre _____

Fecha _____

Hora _____

Practice Workbook **6B–2**

Los quehaceres

Each person below has been given a location from which to do his or her chores. In the spaces provided, list at least two chores each person could logically be doing. Follow the model.

Modelo Alberto y Antonio están en el garaje.

lavan el coche

sacan la basura

limpian el garaje

1. Dolores está en el baño.

_____

_____

_____

2. Eugenio está en el dormitorio.

_____

_____

_____

3. Carolina y Catarina están en la sala.

_____

_____

_____

4. Vladimir está en el comedor.

_____

_____

_____

5. Ana Gracia está en la cocina.

_____

_____

_____

Realidades (A/B)

Capítulo 6B

Nombre _____

Fecha _____

Hora _____

Practice Workbook **6B–3**

La lista de quehaceres

Melisa's mom has left her a list of the things that she has to do before her relatives come over for a dinner party. Complete the list with the appropriate word or phrase. Follow the model.

Modelo ___*Arregla*___ tu cuarto.

1. _____ la mesa del comedor.

2. Tienes que _____ porque no tienes ropa limpia.

3. _____ porque no tenemos platos limpios.

4. ¿Puedes _____? Hay demasiada basura.

5. _____ los platos en la cocina.

6. Necesitas _____ porque el coche está sucio.

7. Hay que _____ porque hay mucho polvo en el primer piso.

8. _____ las camas.

9. ¿Puedes _____ por las alfombras?

10. El baño no está limpio. Necesitas _____ .

11. _____ de comer al perro.

12. Si tienes tiempo, _____ todos los quehaceres.

Go Online WEB CODE jcd-0612
PHSchool.com

Realidades A/B

Capítulo 6B

Nombre _____

Hora _____

Fecha _____

Practice Workbook **6B–4**

No es correcto

The following statements do not make sense. Rewrite the sentences by replacing the underlined words or phrases with words or phrases that make sense. Follow the model.

Modelo Nunca <u>haces</u> en casa cuando tienes quehaceres.
Nunca ayudas en casa cuando tienes quehaceres _____.

1. Tengo que <u>dar</u> la aspiradora por las alfombras.

_____

2. El cuarto está <u>limpio</u>. Voy a limpiarlo.

_____

3. Papá va a lavar platos en <u>el dormitorio</u>.

_____

4. No te <u>recibo</u> dinero porque no estás haciendo nada.

_____

5. ¡<u>Haz la cama!</u> Vamos a comer.

_____

6. Mamá lava <u>el coche</u> en la cocina.

_____

7. ¿Cuáles son los <u>dinero</u> que tienes que hacer?

_____

8. Doy <u>dinero</u> al perro todos los días.

_____

9. Debes cortar <u>el polvo</u>, está bastante largo.

_____

10. Ernesto quita <u>el coche</u> de la sala.

_____

11. Las hermanas <u>cocinan</u> la basura por la noche.

_____

Los mandatos

A. Write the affirmative **tú** command forms of the following verbs in the spaces provided.

1. correr _____

2. poner _____

3. hacer _____

4. comer _____

5. hablar _____

6. leer _____

7. limpiar _____

8. ver _____

9. cortar _____

10. abrir _____

11. escribir _____

B. Now, write the chore your parents might tell you to do in each of the following situations. Follow the model.

| Modelo | Tu dormitorio no está limpio. | *Arregla tu dormitorio* . |

1. El coche está sucio. _____.

2. El perro tiene hambre. _____.

3. No hay platos limpios. _____.

4. Hay mucha basura en el garaje. _____.

5. La camisa blanca ahora es gris. _____.

6. Necesitamos cenar. _____.

7. El baño no está limpio. _____.

8. Hay mucho polvo en la sala. _____.

Realidades A/B

Capítulo 6B

Nombre _____

Fecha _____

Hora _____

Practice Workbook **6B–6**

¿Qué están haciendo?

The Duarte family is getting ready for a barbecue. Look at the picture, then write what each of the family members is doing. Follow the model.

Modelo La madre *está cocinando las hamburguesas* _____.

1. Manolo y José _____.

2. Ana María _____.

3. El padre _____.

4. Tito y Ramón _____.

5. Graciela _____.

6. Lola y Elia _____.

7. Todos _____.

Macho trabajo

The Escobar family is getting ready to have guests over. Fill in the blanks in their conversation below with the appropriate form of the following verbs: **cortar, ayudar, hacer, lavar, pasar, sacar.**

PABLO: Mamá, ¿qué estás _____ tú?

MAMÁ: Estoy _____ los platos, hijo. ¿Y tú?

PABLO: Nada.

MAMÁ: Vale. ¿Qué están _____ tus hermanos?

PABLO: Juan está _____ el baño y Marta está arreglando

su dormitorio.

MAMÁ: Bien, hijo. Ahora, quita el polvo de la sala y luego _____

la aspiradora por las alfombras.

PABLO: Pero, mamá …

MAMÁ: ¡Ahora! Y después _____ la basura …

¡María! ¿Qué estás _____ , hija?

MARÍA: Isabel y yo _____ el césped. ¿Por qué?

MAMÁ: Porque tus primos vienen a comer hoy y necesito ayuda para poner la mesa.

MARÍA: ¿Por qué no te está _____ papá?

MAMÁ: Papá, cariño, ¿dónde estás?

PAPÁ: Estoy en el garaje. Estoy _____ el coche.

MAMÁ: Ah, sí. Después, arregla nuestro cuarto y _____ tu ropa sucia.

PAPÁ: ¿Por qué?

MAMÁ: ¡Vienen tu hermano y su familia!

Go Online WEB CODE jcd-0615
PHSchool.com

Realidades A/B

Capítulo 6B

Nombre _____

Fecha _____

Hora _____

Practice Workbook **6B–8**

Repaso

Across

4. cómo pasas al primer piso desde la planta baja; la ____

6. Yo ____ el baño

9.

12. *to cook*

15. El hijo ____ la aspiradora cada fin de semana.

16.

____ el cuarto

17. La hija debe ____ los platos ahora.

18. un cuarto donde puedes poner el coche

20. cuarto donde come la familia; el ____

21. el piso debajo de la planta baja

Down

1. el cuarto donde preparas la comida

2. Tengo que ____ la cama hoy.

3.

quitar el ____

5.

____ la basura

6. no cerca

7. Después de subir la escalera, estás en el ____ ____.

8. Cuando entras en la casa, estás en la ____ ____.

10. la oficina en la casa

11. ¿Quién va a ____ la mesa?

13. el cuarto donde ves la tele

14. el cuarto donde duermes

19. Mateo tiene que cortar el ____.

21. no limpio

Realidades A/B

Capítulo 6B

Nombre _____

Hora _____

Fecha _____

Practice Workbook **6B–9**

Organizer

I. Vocabulary

Rooms of the house

_____

_____

_____

_____

_____

_____

_____

_____

Outdoor chores

_____

_____

_____

_____

Indoor household tasks

_____

_____

_____

_____

_____

_____

Floors of the house

_____

_____

_____

_____

II. Grammar

1. To talk about actions in progress, use the _____ tense.
   This is formed by adding -_____ to the roots of **-ar** verbs and -_____
   to the roots of **-er** and **-ir** verbs.

2. **Tú** commands are the same as the _____ form of the
   _____ tense of verbs. But the **tú** command form of **poner** is
   _____ and of **hacer** is _____.

Go Online WEB CODE jcd-0616
PHSchool.com

Realidades A/B

Capítulo 7A

Nombre _____

Fecha _____

Hora _____

Practice Workbook **7A–1**

En el escaparate (*store window*)

You are window shopping at a large department store and you decide to make a list of what they have and what everything costs. Using the picture, list seven items and their prices below. Follow the model.

Modelo *Los pantalones cuestan 35 dólares.*

1. _____

2. _____

3. _____

4. _____

5. _____

6. _____

7. _____

Realidades A/B

Capítulo 7A

Nombre _____

Fecha _____

Hora _____

Practice Workbook **7A–2**

Tienda de la Gracia

A. Write the numbers below in Spanish.

1. 100 _____

2. 500 _____

3. 909 _____

4. 222 _____

5. 767 _____

6. 676 _____

7. 110 _____

8. 881 _____

B. Read the following statistics about the chain of stores **Tienda de la Gracia**. Then answer the questions that follow.

TIENDA DE LA GRACIA	
Tiendas	100
Trabajadores	324
Promedio diario (*daily average*) de clientes	760
Camisas	612
Pantalones	404

1. ¿Cuántas Tiendas de la Gracia hay?

_____

2. ¿Cuál es el promedio diario de clientes en cada tienda?

_____

3. ¿Cuántos trabajadores hay en las Tiendas de la Gracia?

_____

4. ¿Cuántos pantalones hay en cada tienda?

_____

5. ¿Y camisas?

_____

Go Online WEB CODE jcd-0701
PHSchool.com

En el centro comercial

Tatiana and Mariana are in the local mall. Write the words that most logically complete their conversation as they go from store to store.

TATIANA: Vamos a esta tienda de ropa. Aquí tienen _____ elegante.

MARIANA: Bien. ¿Qué _____ comprar?

TATIANA: Necesito un vestido para la fiesta de mi primo.

DEPENDIENTA: ¿En qué puedo _____, señorita?

TATIANA: _____ un vestido elegante.

DEPENDIENTA: ¿Va Ud. a _____ el vestido a una fiesta o un baile formal?

TATIANA: A una fiesta. Me gusta este vestido.

MARIANA: ¿Cómo te _____?

TATIANA: ¡Me queda fantástico! Quiero comprarlo.

MARIANA: Vamos a otra tienda. Necesito _____ unos zapatos

nuevos. Vamos a esa tienda, tienen buenos precios allí.

TATIANA: Mira estos zapatos aquí.

MARIANA: ¿Cuánto cuestan?

TATIANA: Trescientos dólares. ¿Es un buen _____?

MARIANA: Sí. Y me quedan _____. Voy a comprar estos zapatos.

TATIANA: Bien. Pasamos a otra tienda.

MARIANA: La tienda de música está a la derecha. ¿Entramos?

TATIANA: Sí, ¡ _____!

Realidades A/B

Capítulo 7A

Nombre _____

Fecha _____

Hora _____

Practice Workbook **7A–4**

¿Qué llevan?

In complete sentences, describe two articles of clothing that each of the people below is wearing.

Pedro

A. _____

_____

B. _____

1. _____

Las hermanas Guzmán

A. _____

_____

B. _____

2. _____

La profesora Jones

A. _____

_____

B. _____

3. _____

El Dr. Cambambia

A. _____

_____

B. _____

4. _____

Anita

A. _____

_____

B. _____

5. _____

Go Online WEB CODE jcd-0702
PHSchool.com

Realidades **A/B**

Capítulo 7A

Nombre _____

Fecha _____

Hora _____

Practice Workbook **7A–5**

Algunos verbos nuevos

A. Fill in the chart below with the forms of the stem-changing verbs indicated.

	PENSAR	QUERER	PREFERIR
yo	*pienso*		
tú			*prefieres*
él, ella, Ud.		*quiere*	
nosotros			*preferimos*
vosotros	*pensáis*	*queréis*	*preferís*
ellos, ellas, Uds.		*quieren*	

B. Now, complete each sentence below by choosing the correct form of the verb **pensar**, **querer**, or **preferir**.

1. ¿_____ (tú) la camisa roja o la camisa azul?

2. Nosotros _____ comprar un suéter nuevo.

3. Ellas _____ ir de compras hoy.

4. Vivian _____ llevar ropa elegante.

5. ¿Uds. _____ trabajar en la tienda de Mónica?

6. Yo _____ comprar los zapatos ahora.

7. Mis amigos y yo _____ jugar al fútbol cuando llueve.

8. Eduardo _____ ir a la fiesta con Brenda.

9. ¿Qué _____ (tú) hacer después de la escuela?

10. Marcelo y Claudio _____ ir al gimnasio después de la escuela.

11. Yo _____ buscar una bicicleta nueva.

12. ¿Tomás va a la tienda o _____ quedarse en casa?

Realidades A/B

Capítulo 7A

Nombre _____

Fecha _____

Hora _____

Practice Workbook **7A–6**

¿Cuál prefieres?

A. Fill in the chart below with the singular and plural, masculine and feminine forms of the demonstrative adjectives.

este		estos	
	esa		esas

B. Complete the following questions about the clothing items pictured by writing in the appropriate demonstrative adjectives from the chart above. Then answer the questions by saying that you prefer the item indicated by the arrow.

1.

—¿Prefieres _____ camisa o _____ suéter?

— _____

— _____

2.

—¿Prefieres _____ pantalones cortos o _____ jeans?

— _____

— _____

3.

—¿Te gustan más _____ sudaderas aquí o _____ suéteres?

— _____

— _____

4.

—¿Te gusta más _____ vestido o _____ falda?

— _____

— _____

5.

—¿Quieres _____ zapatos negros o _____ botas negras?

— _____

— _____

6.

—¿Prefieres _____ chaqueta o _____ abrigo?

— _____

— _____

Go **O**nline WEB CODE jcd-0703
PHSchool.com

Realidades A/B

Capítulo 7A

Nombre _____

Hora _____

Fecha _____

Practice Workbook **7A–7**

¿Quién?

Two sales associates are discussing some of the clients in their busy store. Fill in the blanks with the appropriate demonstrative adjectives based on the picture.

CELIA: ¿Qué hace _____ mujer allá?

YOLANDA: Pues, está mirando las botas, pero no quiere pagar mucho.

CELIA: ¿Qué quieren _____ mujeres aquí?

YOLANDA: Piensan comprar unos calcetines.

CELIA: ¿Y _____ hombre solo allí?

YOLANDA: ¿_____ hombre? Prefiere mirar los pantalones.

CELIA: A la derecha de él hay unos niños, ¿no? ¿Qué hacen _____ niños?

YOLANDA: Pues, _____ niños quieren unos suéteres nuevos.

CELIA: Oye, ¿ves a _____ hombres al lado de la puerta?

YOLANDA: Sí, piensan comprar _____ abrigos. ¿Por qué?

CELIA: Pues, son muy guapos, ¿no?

YOLANDA: Ah, sí. Creo que necesitan ayuda.

CELIA: ¡Hasta luego!

WEB CODE jcd-0705

Manos a la obra ━ *Gramática* **127**

Realidades A/B

Capítulo 7A

Nombre _____

Fecha _____

Hora _____

Practice Workbook **7A–8**

Repaso

Down

1.

2.

Across

2. Llevas ____ debajo de los zapatos.

3. ____ de baño

6. ¿Te ____ bien ese suéter?

7.

8. los ____ cortos

10. Yo llevo ____ en los pies.

12. No cuestan tanto. Es un buen ____.

14. En esta tienda, quiero ____ unas botas.

15. Jaime es informal. Siempre lleva camiseta y los ____.

17. Ella tiene que comprar un ____ para la fiesta.

18.

4. ¿Cuánto ____ las botas?

5. Mi padre es inteligente. Siempre tiene ____.

6. 5000 ÷ 10

8. ____, señorita. Necesito ayuda.

9. Llevo una ____ en la cabeza.

11. Cuando hace frío, llevo un ____.

13. la ____ de ropa

16. 500 x 2

Realidades A/B

Capítulo 7A

Nombre _____

Hora _____

Fecha _____

Practice Workbook **7A–9**

Organizer

I. Vocabulary

Clothing for warm weather

_____

_____

_____

_____

Clothing for cold weather

_____

_____

_____

_____

_____

_____

Other words to talk about clothing

_____

_____

_____

Numbers in the hundreds

_____

_____

_____

_____

_____

_____

II. Grammar

1. The forms of the verb **pensar** are: _____ _____

    _____ _____

    _____ _____

    The forms of the verb **querer** are: _____ _____

    _____ _____

    _____ _____

    The forms of the verb **preferir** are: _____ _____

    _____ _____

    _____ _____

2. To refer to something close, use _____ / _____, _____ / _____; to refer to something further away, use _____ / _____, _____ / _____.

Realidades A/B

Capítulo 7B

Nombre _____

Fecha _____

Hora _____

Practice Workbook **7B–1**

Los regalos

Marcela is writing a list of gifts she wants to buy for her family. Help her by writing the names of the items suggested by the pictures in the blanks provided.

1. Para mi novio:

_____ _____ _____ _____

2. Para mi mejor amiga:

_____ _____

3. Para mi hermana:

_____ _____ _____ _____

4. Para mi padre:

_____ _____ _____

5. Para mi madre:

_____ _____ _____

Go Online WEB CODE jcd-0711
PHSchool.com

¡Tantas tiendas!

Write the names of the items pictured in the first blank, and where each person would find the items in the second blank.

1. Yo busco _____

   en una _____.

2. Germán busca _____

   en una _____.

3. Tú buscas _____

   en la _____.

4. Mi hermano busca _____

   en la _____.

5. Bárbara busca _____

   en un _____.

6. Buscamos _____

   en la _____.

7. Esteban y Luis buscan un _____

   en la _____.

8. Susana y Paulina buscan _____

   en una _____.

9. —¿En dónde puedo comprar _____?

   —En un _____.

Realidades A/B

Capítulo 7B

Nombre _____

Hora _____

Fecha _____

Practice Workbook **7B–3**

¿El regalo perfecto?

Valentine's Day is coming and Pepe and Laura are deciding what gifts to give each other.

A. Read the conversations below.

(*En una tienda de descuentos*)

PEPE:	Necesito comprar un regalo para mi novia.
DEPENDIENTE:	¿Qué piensa comprar?
PEPE:	No sé. Tiene que ser algo barato porque no tengo mucho dinero.
DEPENDIENTE:	Pero, ¿no quiere un anillo bonito o un collar elegante para su novia?
PEPE:	No. Es demasiado.
DEPENDIENTE:	Puede comprar un reloj pulsera que no cuesta tanto.
PEPE:	Oiga, el mes pasado compré software nuevo para mi computadora, para poder jugar videojuegos en la Red. ¡Pagué unos 90 dólares!
DEPENDIENTE:	Entonces quiere este llavero de veinte dólares.
PEPE:	¡Genial!

(*En un almacén*)

LAURA:	Quiero el regalo perfecto para mi novio.
DEPENDIENTA:	¿Él trabaja? ¿Quizás una corbata bonita?
LAURA:	Estoy pensando en un regalo más romántico . . .
DEPENDIENTA:	¿Unos guantes para las noches de frío?
LAURA:	No creo. Él nunca tiene frío. ¿Ud. tiene algo romántico?
DEPENDIENTA:	¡Mire! ¿Qué piensa de este anillo de cincuenta dólares?
LAURA:	¡Perfecto! Quiero uno, por favor.

B. Answer the questions about the dialogues in complete sentences.

1. ¿A qué tienda va Pepe? _____

   ¿Qué busca allí? ¿Por qué? _____

   _____

2. ¿Qué quiere venderle el dependiente? ¿Por qué Pepe no quiere comprarlos?

   _____

   _____

3. ¿Qué compra por fin Pepe? _____

4. ¿Qué quiere comprar Laura? _____

5. ¿Por qué Laura no quiere ni una corbata ni unos guantes? _____

   _____

6. ¿Qué va a comprar Laura? _____ ¿Es más

   caro o más barato que el regalo de Pepe? _____

Go Online WEB CODE jcd-0712
PHSchool.com

Realidades A/B

Capítulo 7B

Nombre _____

Fecha _____

Hora _____

Practice Workbook **7B–4**

Oraciones desordenadas

Put the scrambled sentences below into logical order.

1. compré / hace / lo / semana / una

_____

2. yo / por / ayer / unos / pagué / un / guantes / dólar

_____

3. lector / caro / DVD / un / es / muy / no

_____

4. joyas / en / venden / almacén / el

_____

5. pasada / la / compré / yo / semana / suéter / nuevo / un

_____

6. anoche / una / compré / computadora / yo / nueva

_____

7. pagaste / el / collar / cuánto / por

¿_____?

8. lo / año / el / tú / compraste / pasado

_____

9. joyas / por / venden / tienda / esta / veinte / en / dólares

_____

10. cuánto / por / el / pagaste / reloj

¿_____?

Realidades (A/B)

Capítulo 7B

Nombre _____

Hora _____

Fecha _____

Practice Workbook **7B–5**

Hablamos del pasado

A. Fill in the chart below with the preterite forms of the verbs indicated.

	COMPRAR	HABLAR	PREPARAR	USAR	MIRAR
yo	compré				
tú					miraste
él, ella, Ud.		habló			
nosotros				usamos	
vosotros	comprasteis	hablasteis	preparasteis	usasteis	mirasteis
ellos, ellas, Uds.			prepararon		

B. Fill in the blanks in the following postcard with the correct preterite forms of the verbs given.

¡Hola, mamá!

   ¿Cómo estás? Estoy muy bien aquí en Quito.
Primero, José y yo _____ (preparar) unos
sándwiches ricos y _____ (hablar) con su
mamá un poco. Después, decidimos ir al centro
comercial. José y su mamá _____ (mirar)
unas chaquetas en la tienda de Smith y yo
_____ (comprar) algunas cosas para la
semana.

   A las cinco, la mamá de José _____
(llamar) por teléfono al padre, y él _____
(regresar) del trabajo un poco después. Nosotros
_____ (cenar) y _____ (usar) la
computadora antes de dormir.

   ¿Y tú? ¿_____ (caminar) esta semana?
¿_____ (comprar) el regalo para el
cumpleaños de papi? Pues, nos vemos en una semana.
¡Mañana me voy a Lima!

                        Un abrazo,
                        Victor

La Sra. Guiraldo
Vía Águila 1305
Col. Cuauhtémoc
06500 México, D.F.

Go Online WEB CODE jcd-0713
PHSchool.com

Realidades (A/B)

Capítulo 7B

Nombre _____

Hora _____

Fecha _____

Practice Workbook **7B–6**

Mini-conversaciones

A. Fill in the following charts with the preterite forms of the verbs given.

	PAGAR	BUSCAR	JUGAR	PRACTICAR	TOCAR
yo	pagué			practiqué	
tú			jugaste		
él, ella, Ud.		buscó			
nosotros					tocamos
vosotros	pagasteis	buscasteis	jugasteis	practicasteis	tocasteis
ellos, ellas, Uds.				practicaron	

B. Now, complete the mini-conversations below with preterite verb forms from the chart above.

1. —Juan, ¿cuánto _____ por tu suéter?

   —Yo _____ 25 dólares.

2. —¿Qué hizo Marta anoche?

   —Ella _____ al fútbol con sus hermanos.

3. —Hija, ¿_____ el piano?

   —Sí, mamá. _____ por una hora.

4. —Busco un apartamento nuevo.

   —Yo _____ por un año antes de encontrar el apartamento perfecto.

5. —¿Uds. _____ un instrumento en el pasado?

   —Sí, nosotros _____ el violín.

6. —¿Marcos va a practicar el básquetbol hoy?

   —No, él _____ toda la semana pasada.

7. —¿Con quién _____ (tú) al golf?

   —_____ con mis dos hermanos y con mi padre.

Objeto directo

A. Rewrite the following sentences about shopping using direct object pronouns in place of the appropriate nouns.

1. Compré los zapatos. _____

2. ¿Tienes el vestido verde? _____

3. Escribo el cuento. _____

4. Mi mamá recibe el dinero. _____

5. Las mujeres llevan las faldas nuevas. _____

6. ¿Rosario va a comprar el regalo? _____

7. Las amigas compraron aretes nuevos. _____

8. Llevo los dos abrigos. _____

B. Ramona's mother is talking to her about their trip to the mall. Answer her questions using direct object pronouns. Follow the model.

Modelo ¿Llevas tu vestido nuevo a la escuela?

Sí, lo llevo mucho. _____

1. ¿Dónde vas a poner tu camisa nueva?

_____

2. ¿Compraste los zapatos azules?

_____

3. ¿Usas el reloj pulsera negro?

_____

4. ¿Cuándo vas a llevar tus guantes nuevos?

_____

5. ¿Tienes las camisetas nuevas?

_____

Go Online WEB CODE jcd-0715
PHSchool.com

Realidades A/B

Capítulo 7B

Nombre _____

Hora _____

Fecha _____

Practice Workbook **7B–8**

Repaso

Across

5. donde las mujeres ponen las llaves, bolígrafos, etc.

7. la ____ de electrodomésticos

8. tienda donde venden zapatos

13.

14. los ____ de sol

17. Una tienda de ropa es donde ____ ropa.

18. no caro

20. tienda donde venden joyas

Down

1. Llevo los ____ durante el invierno porque tengo las manos frías.

2. Sancho quiere ____ las fotos de tu viaje.

3.

4. donde pones el dinero y a veces unas fotos; la ____

6. tienda donde venden libros

9. joya que llevas en las orejas

10. tienda donde venden todo

11. tipo de reloj que llevas en el cuerpo; reloj ____

12. donde pones las llaves

15. joya que llevas en el dedo

16. Los hombres llevan una camisa con ____ al trabajo.

19. *last night*

Realidades A/B

Capítulo 7B

Nombre _____

Hora _____

Fecha _____

Practice Workbook **7B–9**

Organizer

I. Vocabulary

Types of stores

_____

_____

_____

_____

_____

_____

Words to talk about jewelry

_____

_____

_____

_____

_____

_____

Other gifts

_____

_____

_____

_____

Words to talk about the past

_____

_____

_____

_____

_____

II. Grammar

1. The preterite endings of **-ar** verbs are: -_____   -_____

   -_____   -_____

   -_____   -_____

   Now conjugate the verb **pasar** in the preterite: _____   _____

   _____   _____

   _____   _____

2. The preterite ending of the **yo** form of verbs ending with **-car** is -_____ . For
   -gar verbs it is -_____ .

3. The direct object pronouns are _____ , _____ , _____ , and
   _____ .

Go Online WEB CODE jcd-0717
PHSchool.com

¿Adónde van?

Complete the mini-conversations. Use the drawing to fill in the first blank and to give you a clue for the second blank. Follow the model.

Modelo

—¿Viste el ____monumento____ nuevo de Cristóbal Colón?

—Sí, ¡es fantástico! Está enfrente del ____museo____.

1. —Mamá, quiero ver _____.

—Sí, Marisol. Vamos al _____.

2. —¿Uds. van de vacaciones en _____ este verano?

—No, vamos a la _____.

3. —¿Vas a ver _____ hoy?

—Sí, mis padres y yo vamos al _____.

4. —¿Quieres _____ hoy?

—Sí, pero ¿en dónde? ¿En el _____?

5. —¿Dónde es el _____?

—Pues, en el _____, por supuesto.

6. —¿Cómo te gusta ir de _____?

—Siempre viajamos en _____.

Asociaciones

A. Write the names of the places from your vocabulary that you associate with the following things or actions.

1. la historia, el arte ___ ___ ___ (◯) ___ ___ ___ (◯) ___

2. las atracciones, los monos ___ ___ ___ (◯) ___ ___ ___ ___

3. pintar, dibujar, el arte ___ ___ (◯) ___ ___

4. divertido, personas atrevidas, jugar ___ ___ (◯) ___ ___ ___ ___ ___

   ___ ___ ___ (◯) ___ ___ ___ (◯) ___

5. los deportes, un partido, ver (◯) ___ ___ ___ (◯) ___ ___

6. la obra, el actor ___ (◯) ___ ___ ___ ___

7. el hotel, muchas personas (◯) ___ ___ ___ ___ ___ ___

8. pasear en bote, mucha agua ___ ___ ___ (◯) ___

B. Now, unscramble the circled letters to find a related word.

___ ___ ___ ___ ___ ___ ___ ___ ___ ___ ___

Go Online WEB CODE jcd-0801
PHSchool.com

Realidades A/B

Capítulo 8A

Nombre _____

Hora _____

Fecha _____

Practice Workbook **8A–3**

¡Vamos al parque nacional!

The Carreras family went on vacation to Rocky Mountain National Park in Colorado. Read the postcard they sent to their friends back home and fill in the blanks with the words suggested by the pictures.

¡Saludos desde Colorado!

Llegamos al _____ el lunes pasado. Yo fui directamente

a la playa para _____ . El _____

es precioso y ¡los _____ son enormes! El martes paseamos

en _____ por el lago y miramos los _____

. ¡Yo vi un oso en el bosque!

Para mañana tenemos muchos planes. Vamos a _____

por las montañas y por la noche vamos al _____ para ver

una obra musical.

Regresamos a la _____ el viernes. ¡Nos vemos

este fin de semana!

Abrazos,

Familia Carreras

¿Qué te pasó?

A. Read the dialogue between Aníbal and Carmen about Aníbal's trip to the beach.

CARMEN: Dime, ¿fuiste a la playa con tus primos?

ANÍBAL: ¡Ay, amiga; fue un desastre! Salí muy temprano para pasar todo el día allí.

Durante el día tomamos el sol y buceamos en el mar.

CARMEN: ¿No fue un día tremendo para descansar y pasarlo bien con tus amigos?

ANÍBAL: Por dos horas, sí. Pero después de mucha lluvia, todo salió mal.

CARMEN: Lo siento. Va a hacer buen tiempo este sábado. . .

ANÍBAL: Bueno, tú y yo podemos salir de la ciudad.

CARMEN: ¡Genial!

B. Now, answer the questions in complete sentences.

1. ¿Adónde fue Aníbal? _____

_____

2. ¿Qué hizo allí? _____

_____

3. ¿Con quién fue Aníbal? _____

_____

4. ¿Qué tiempo va a hacer el sábado? _____

_____

5. ¿Qué van a hacer Aníbal y Carmen? _____

_____

Go Online WEB CODE jcd-0802
PHSchool.com

Realidades A/B

Capítulo 8A

Nombre _____

Fecha _____

Hora _____

Practice Workbook **8A–5**

¿Qué hicieron?

A. Fill in the chart with the preterite forms of the verbs given.

	COMER	ESCRIBIR	CORRER	SALIR	VER	BEBER
yo	comí				vi	
tú			corriste			
él, ella, Ud.				salió		bebió
nosotros		escribimos				
vosotros	comisteis	escribisteis	corristeis	salisteis	visteis	bebisteis
ellos/as, Uds.						

B. Now, complete the mini-conversations below by filling in the appropriate forms of one of the verbs from Part A.

1. —Pablo, ¿vas a correr hoy?

   —No, _____ ayer.

2. —¿Elena _____ toda la leche?

   —Sí, toda.

3. —¿Uds. salieron anoche?

   —Sí, _____ a las once.

4. —¿_____ la nueva película de Almodóvar?

   —Sí, la vi anoche.

5. —¡Qué buenos niños!

   —Sí, _____ todas las zanahorias.

6. —Juan, escribe la tarea.

   —Ya la _____, mamá.

7. —¿Uds. comieron en el hotel anoche?

   —No, _____ en el restaurante.

8. —¿Quién va a correr en el maratón este año?

   —Todos, porque sólo dos personas _____ el año pasado.

9. —¿Con quién saliste, Marta?

   —_____ con Toño.

10. —¿El autor va a escribir un cuento nuevo?

    —No, él _____ uno el mes pasado.

¿Adónde fueron?

Some friends are talking about where they went on vacation. Write where they went, using the pictures below to help you. Follow the model.

 **Modelo** La familia Madrigal *fue al zoológico* _____.

 **1.** Carlos _____.

 **2.** Yo _____.

 **3.** Lola y Tina _____.

 **4.** Nosotros _____.

 **5.** Elisa _____.

 **6.** Tú _____.

7. Uds. _____.

Go Online WEB CODE jcd-0804
PHSchool.com

Realidades A/B

Capítulo 8A

Nombre _____

Hora _____

Fecha _____

Practice Workbook **8A–7**

¿Qué viste?

Alicia saw many things at the park yesterday. Use the drawing and the location clues to say whom or what she saw. Pay attention to the use of the personal **a** in your statements. Follow the model.

| **Modelo** | En el parque ayer, yo vi ___*a unos amigos*___ corriendo. |

1. Yo vi _____ dándoles de comer a unos pájaros.

2. Yo vi _____ jugando al fútbol.

3. Yo vi _____ en la mesa.

4. En el lago, yo vi _____ paseando.

5. En el bote, yo vi _____ con una señorita.

6. En un árbol yo vi _____.

7. Al lado del árbol vi _____.

8. Debajo del árbol vi _____ con pelo largo.

9. En la playa vi _____.

Realidades **A/B**

Capítulo 8A

Nombre _____

Hora _____

Fecha _____

Practice Workbook **8A-8**

Repaso

Down

1. Me gusta ___ en el sofá.
2. donde puedes pasear en bote; el ___
3. Yo quiero ___ la tele.
4. medio de transporte que va por el agua; el ___
5. un edificio con muchos cuadros; el ___
8. medio de transporte que usan los estudiantes para ir a la escuela; el ___
10. la ___ de teatro
12. *the train;* el ___
13. *the sea;* el ___
14. sinónimo de **vacaciones**; un ___

17.

20. Chicago es una ___ donde hace mucho viento.

22.

Across

2. *place;* un ___
6. En el monumento, compramos ___.
7. el ___ de diversiones

9.

11. donde se juegan los partidos de fútbol; el ___
15. España es un ___ donde hablan español.
16. medio de transporte que va por el aire; el ___
18. pasear en ___
19. donde hay atracciones de animales; el ___
21. no tarde

Organizer

I. Vocabulary

Places to visit

_____

_____

_____

_____

_____

Modes of transportation

_____

_____

_____

_____

Leisure activities

_____

_____

_____

_____

Phrases to discuss experiences

_____

_____

_____

_____

II. Grammar

1. The preterite endings of **-er** and **-ir** verbs are:

yo   -_____   nosotros -_____

tú   -_____   vosotros -_isteis___

Ud. -_____   Uds.   -_____

2. The preterite forms of **ir** (and **ser**) are: _____ _____

_____ _____

_____ _____

3. _____ is inserted before the direct object of a sentence if the direct object is

a person. This is called the _____.

Realidades A/B

Capítulo 8B

Nombre _____

Fecha _____

Hora _____

Practice Workbook **8B–1**

La comunidad

Your new friend in Costa Rica is showing you around her community. Label each place or point of interest in the picture with the appropriate word.

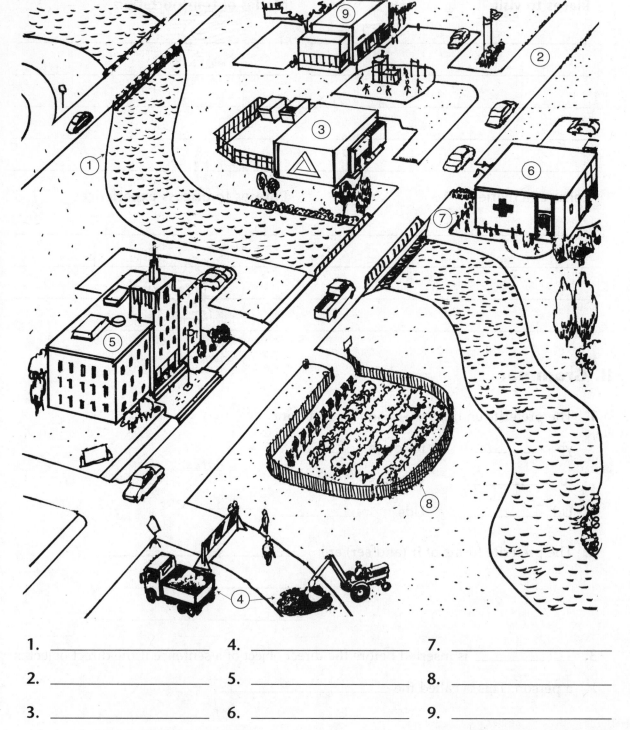

1. _____   4. _____   7. _____

2. _____   5. _____   8. _____

3. _____   6. _____   9. _____

Go Online WEB CODE jcd-0811
PHSchool.com

Realidades A/B

Capítulo 8B

Nombre _____

Fecha _____

Hora _____

Practice Workbook **8B–2**

El reciclaje

A. Your community is starting a recycling program. Label each item below with words from your vocabulary.

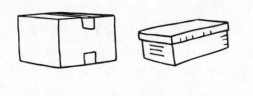

1. _____

4. _____

2. _____

5. la botella de _____

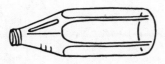

3. _____

6. la botella de _____

B. Now, write sentences to say whether or not it is necessary to recycle the items below. Follow the model.

Modelo Los tomates *No es necesario reciclar los tomates.* _____

1. El helado _____

2. El plástico _____

3. El vidrio _____

4. La sala _____

5. Las latas _____

Realidades A/B

Capítulo 8B

Nombre _____

Hora _____

Fecha _____

Practice Workbook **8B–3**

El voluntario

A. Read the letter below from Álvaro, who is working as an AmeriCorps volunteer.

Querida familia:

¡Qué experiencia! Hacemos tantas cosas para ayudar a los demás. La semana pasada ayudamos en un proyecto de construcción con otro grupo de voluntarios. Ellos van a terminar el proyecto. Después de eso, fuimos a un centro de reciclaje. Allí aprendimos a reciclar el papel y el vidrio. También nos enseñaron cómo separar el papel normal (como el papel de los libros) de los periódicos.

Esta semana nosotros recogimos mucha ropa usada de varias partes de la ciudad y la llevamos a un centro para pobres. Allí le dimos la ropa a la gente pobre del barrio.

Hoy vamos a un centro para ancianos para ayudar a personas mayores. Estoy cansado, pero es importante hacer esto.

¡Hasta pronto!

Álvaro

B. Now, answer the questions below.

1. ¿Cuántas cosas hace Álvaro para ayudar a los demás? ¿Cuáles son? _____

_____

_____

2. ¿Qué aprendió Álvaro en el centro de reciclaje? _____

_____

3. ¿Adónde llevaron Álvaro y los voluntarios la ropa usada? _____

_____

4. ¿A quiénes le dieron la ropa? _____

_____

5. ¿Qué hace Álvaro hoy? _____

_____

¿Qué haces en la comunidad?

You overhear two friends telling their teacher about what they do to help out in their communities. You can't hear what the teacher is asking. Fill in the teacher's questions. Follow the model.

Modelo   —*¿Uds. ayudan en la comunidad?* _____

—Sí, trabajamos como voluntarios en la comunidad.

—¿ _____ ?

—Trabajamos en una escuela primaria. Les enseñamos a los niños a leer.

—¿ _____ ?

—También recogemos ropa usada.

—¿ _____ ?

—Recogemos la ropa usada del barrio.

—¿ _____ ?

—Hay que separar la ropa y después lavarla.

—¿ _____ ?

—Le damos la ropa usada a la gente pobre del barrio.

—¿ _____ ?

—Sí, ayudamos en el hospital.

—¿ _____ ?

—Trabajamos como voluntarios en un hospital para niños. Nos encanta el trabajo voluntario.

¿Quién dice qué?

The people in the chart below are concerned citizens. Tell what each says by combining the subject on the left with the phrase on the right using **decir** + **que**. Follow the model.

Subjects	Phrases
Smokey the Bear	Hay que tener cuidado en el campamento.
Los directores del centro de reciclaje	Es necesario separar el plástico y el vidrio.
Gloria	La gente tiene que limpiar el barrio.
Yo	Todos deben participar en las actividades de la comunidad.
La profesora	Es esencial hacer trabajo voluntario.
La Cruz Roja	Es importante ayudar a los enfermos.
Tú	Es importante llevar la ropa usada a centros para los pobres.
Mi familia y yo	Es importante reciclar las botellas y latas.

Modelo *Smokey the Bear dice que hay que tener cuidado en el campamento.*

1. _____

2. _____

3. _____

4. _____

5. _____

6. _____

7. _____

Go Online WEB CODE jcd-0813
PHSchool.com

Realidades A/B

Capítulo 8B

Nombre _____

Fecha _____

Hora _____

Practice Workbook **8B–6**

Más trabajo voluntario

A. Write the indirect object pronouns that correspond to the following phrases.

1. A Javier y a Sara _____

2. A Diego y a mí _____

3. A la Dra. Estes _____

4. A Uds. _____

5. A Tito _____

6. A Luz y a ti _____

7. A ti _____

8. A nosotros _____

9. Al Sr. Pérez _____

10. A mí _____

B. Now, fill in the blanks in the following sentences with the correct indirect object pronouns.

1. La Cruz Roja _____ ayuda a las personas de la comunidad.

2. Nuestros padres _____ hablaron a mi hermano y a mí del reciclaje.

3. Mi profesora _____ ayudó a decidir qué trabajo voluntario me gustaría hacer.

4. _____ dice el profesor al estudiante que es importante separar las latas y el plástico.

5. Las personas _____ escriben al director del centro de reciclaje para recibir información sobre el reciclaje.

6. ¿Tus padres _____ dicen que debes ayudar a los demás?

7. _____ traigo unos juguetes a los niños en el hospital.

8. Los ancianos están muy contentos cuando _____ decimos que volvemos mañana.

¿Hacer o dar?

A. Fill in the chart below with the correct forms of **hacer** and **dar** in the preterite.

	HACER	DAR
yo	*hice*	*di*
tú		
él, ella, Ud.		
nosotros		
vosotros	*hicisteis*	*disteis*
ellos, ellas, Uds.		

B. Now, fill in the blanks in the telephone conversation below with the appropriate forms from the chart above.

LEYDIN: ¡Mamá, estoy aquí en los Estados Unidos!

MADRE: Hola, hija. ¿Cómo estás?

LEYDIN: Bien, mamá. Yo _____ muchas cosas ayer después de llegar.

MADRE: ¿Qué _____?

LEYDIN: Pues, primero les _____ los regalos a toda la familia.

MADRE: ¿Y la abuelita te _____ un regalo a ti, también?

LEYDIN: Sí, ¡una bicicleta nueva! Estoy muy contenta.

MADRE: Y, ¿qué _____ Uds. después?

LEYDIN: Los primos _____ la tarea y la abuelita y yo le _____ la lista de cosas que comprar para la cena. Después le _____ la lista al abuelo, quien _____ las compras en el supermercado.

MADRE: ¿_____ Uds. algo más?

LEYDIN: Sí. Después de comer, yo _____ un postre especial para todos: ¡tu famoso pastel de tres leches!

MADRE: ¡Qué coincidencia! Yo _____ uno también y les _____ un poco a nuestros amigos, los Sánchez. ¿Qué más . . .?

Go Online WEB CODE jcd-0814
PHSchool.com

Realidades A/B

Capítulo 8B

Nombre _____

Fecha _____

Hora _____

Practice Workbook **8B-8**

Repaso

Across

2. Es importante ____ las botellas usadas de las calles.

4. Es necesario ayudar a los ____.

6. otra ____

10. *unforgettable*

13. el ____ de construcción

15.

16. lugar donde recogen las verduras y las plantas; el ____

20. AmeriCorps hace el trabajo ____.

22. Esa ____ es de cartón.

24. *problem*

Down

1. *poor*

3. Puedes reciclar una ____ de vidrio o de plástico.

5. *often*; ____ ____

7. Puedes reciclar las botellas de ____ y de plástico.

8. Es importante reciclar las cajas de ____.

9. sinónimo de **las personas**; la ____

11. Los ____ son nuestro futuro.

12. el ____ de reciclaje

13.

14. El profesor ____ las botellas al centro de reciclaje.

17. el ____ Grande

18. *toy*; un ____

19. Mis padres me ____ la verdad.

21. sinónimo de **la comunidad**; el ____

23.

Realidades A/B

Capítulo 8B

Nombre _____

Hora _____

Fecha _____

Practice Workbook **8B–9**

Organizer

I. Vocabulary

Places to do volunteer work

_____

_____

_____

_____

_____

Things that are recyclable

_____

_____

_____

_____

_____

Verbs to talk about recycling

_____

_____

_____

Words to describe experiences

_____

_____

_____

II. Grammar

1. The forms of **decir** in the present are: _____ _____

    _____ _____

    _____ _____

2. The indirect object pronouns are: _____ _____

    _____ _____

    _____ _____

3. The preterite forms of **dar** are: The preterite forms of **hacer** are:

    _____ _____   _____ _____

    _____ _____   _____ _____

    _____ _____   _____ _____

Go Online WEB CODE jcd-0817
PHSchool.com

Realidades A/B

Capítulo 9A

Nombre _____

Fecha _____

Hora _____

Practice Workbook **9A–1**

Las películas

A. You love movies, but always forget to check the newspaper for the showings. You constantly have to ask your friends what movies are showing and at what time. Complete each dialogue by filling in the words that best identify the picture.

1. —¿Cuándo empieza la _____?

   —Empieza a las nueve y media. Son casi las nueve. ¡Vamos ahora!

2. —¿Va a ser larga la _____?

   —Sí. Empieza a las dos y media y termina a las cinco menos cuarto.

3. —¿A qué hora dan la _____?

   —A las seis.

4. —¿Cuánto dura el _____?

   —Dura menos de tres horas.

5. —¿Cuándo va a empezar la _____?

   —Empieza a las cuatro y media.

6. —Ya es la una y veinte. ¿Qué podemos hacer?

   —Podemos ir al cine a ver una _____.

B. Now, say the following time expressions another way using new vocabulary phrases.

1. Son las cinco menos diez. _____.

2. Son las dos y treinta. _____.

3. Dura una hora y cincuenta minutos. Dura _____.

4. Termina a las once y cuarenta. Termina _____.

¿Qué programas les gustan?

Read the information about each person below. Then decide which TV program would be best for him or her and write it in the blank.

1. Pedro es gracioso. Siempre cuenta chistes y hace cosas cómicas. A él le gustan

   los programas _____.

2. Mi padre lee el periódico todos los días. Le interesa la política. A él le gustan

   los programas _____.

3. La profesora tiene dos hijos y quiere enseñarles mucho. También busca información

   para usar en la clase. Ella prefiere los programas _____.

4. Abuela no trabaja y tiene que estar en casa. Le interesan mucho los

   juegos, especialmente cuando la gente gana dinero. A ella le gustan los programas

   _____.

5. Javi toca la guitarra y Juanita canta. Pasan casi todo el tiempo practicando la

   música. A ellos les gustan los programas _____.

6. Rosa estudia inglés. Un día quiere trabajar para un periódico. Para aprender más

   de la gente, ella ve los programas _____.

7. Ronaldo es deportista. Juega al fútbol, al béisbol y al básquetbol. Cuando no está

   practicando un deporte está viendo programas _____.

8. A Cristina le gustan las historias. Lee novelas románticas y a veces escribe cuentos

   de amor. A ella le gustan las _____.

WEB CODE jcd-0901
PHSchool.com

¿Cómo son las cosas allí?

Luzma is writing a letter to her pen pal in the U.S. She is telling her pen pal about TV and movies in her country. Fill in the blanks with the words that best complete her thoughts.

Querida Valerie,

¿Qué tal? ¿Cómo fue la _____ que viste la semana pasada? En

mi país me encanta ir al cine. Me gustan más las películas _____.

Mi hermano es policía y _____ yo sé mucho _____

los policías. También me interesa esta clase de películas porque son más

_____ que una comedia o la ciencia ficción. Las comedias

_____ aburren y a veces son infantiles. No me gustan las películas

de _____ porque son demasiado violentas. ¿Qué _____

película te gusta más a ti?

Ahora te hablo de los _____ de televisión aquí. Bueno, no son

muy diferentes de los programas de allí. Tenemos programas de dibujos

animados como *Rin, ran, run,* programas de _____ como *¡Una*

fortuna para ti! y tenemos las noticias. Yo veo las noticias pero sólo me

interesan los programas que dan sobre la policía en el _____ 56.

Eso es todo. Adiós, amiga.

Luzma

Tus programas favoritos

Read the TV listings below, then answer the questions that follow in complete sentences.

EVENING — NOCHE			
6PM	**2** Noticias	8PM **2** ¡Niágara!	
	18 Amigos	**18** Amigos	
	26 Noticias	**26** Película: El monstruo verde	
	30 Pepito y Paquito	**30** El mundo real	
	33 Mi casa	**33** Hoy día	
	42 Deportivas	**42** Fútbol	
	60 Música cubana	**60** ¿Puedes cantar?	
7pm	**2** Los monos	9PM **2** El zoológico	
	18 Noticias	**18** Mi Amiga Sara	
	26 Entre tú y yo	**26**	
	30 Noticias	**30** El día en Alaska	
	33 Noticias	**33** ¡Ganar un coche!	
	42 Deportes	**42**	
	60 La salsa y la samba	**60** Baile en vivo	

1. ¿Cuántos programas de noticias empiezan a las seis? _____

2. ¿Qué clase de programas tiene el canal 42? _____

   ¿Y el canal 60? _____

   ¿Y el canal 2? _____

3. ¿Qué programa deportivo puedes ver a las ocho? _____

   _____

4. Para ver un programa educativo, ¿vas a ver el canal 2 o el 18 a las nueve? _____

   _____

5. ¿Qué clase de programa empieza a las nueve en el canal 33? _____

   ¿Y a las nueve en el canal 30? _____

6. ¿Qué clase de programa dan a las siete en el canal 26? _____

7. ¿Dan una película de horror a las ocho en el canal 26?

   _____

Realidades A/B

Capítulo 9A

Nombre

Hora

Fecha

Practice Workbook **9A–5**

Acabo de . . .

Write what the following people just finished doing and are now going to do, based on the pictures. Follow the model.

Modelo

Marta _acaba de estudiar. Ahora va a dormir._

1. Anabel _____

_____

2. Nosotros _____

_____

3. Ellas _____

_____

4. Yo _____

_____

5. Tú _____

_____

6. Juan y el Sr. Lebredo _____

_____

7. Roberto _____

_____

8. Ana María _____

_____

Más gustos

A. Complete the sentences below with the correct forms of the verbs given.

1. Al Presidente le _____ (interesar) la política.

2. ¡Qué terrible! Me _____ (doler) el pie izquierdo.

3. A los estudiantes les _____ (aburrir) las presentaciones largas.

4. A nosotros nos _____ (encantar) ver comedias.

5. A tus hermanos les _____ (gustar) las películas de horror.

6. A ti te _____ (interesar) el teatro.

7. Me _____ (quedar) bien los pantalones pero me

   _____ (faltar) el dinero para comprarlos.

B. Now, complete each sentence below with the correct form of the verb given and the appropriate indirect object pronoun. Follow the model.

Modelo A Carlos _____*le aburre*_____ (aburrir) la política.

1. A mí _____ (faltar) un lápiz.

2. A ellas _____ (aburrir) las clases de arte.

3. A Carmen _____ (quedar) bien la falda, ¿no?

4. A ti _____ (encantar) los programas deportivos.

5. ¿A ti y a Pedro _____ (gustar) leer revistas?

6. A mi papá _____ (doler) los pies.

7. ¿A Ud. _____ (faltar) los cuadernos?

8. A nosotros _____ (interesar) las obras de teatro.

9. A Lola y a Roberto _____ (interesar) el programa musical y el programa educativo.

 **Go Online** WEB CODE jcd-0904
PHSchool.com

Realidades A/B

Capítulo 9A

Nombre _____

Hora _____

Fecha _____

Practice Workbook **9A–7**

Frases revueltas

The following sentences are mixed up. Rearrange them so that they are grammatically correct and make sense. Don't forget to conjugate verbs where appropriate. Follow the model.

Modelo   ir al cine / me / a mí / y al centro comercial / gustar

A mí me gusta ir al cine y al centro comercial. _____

1. le / leer / a Elena / poemas / encantar / y escribir

_____

2. negros / unos zapatos / te / para / faltar / a ti / ir a la fiesta

_____

3. diez kilómetros / a mí / doler / después de / me / los pies / correr

_____

4. al Sr. Mirabal / interesar / americano / le / el fútbol

_____

5. los programas / les / a mis padres / de entrevistas / aburrir

_____

6. importar / voluntario / a nosotros / el trabajo / nos

_____

7. a Uds. / los boletos para el cine / les / para comprar / faltar / el dinero

_____

8. interesar / les / a José y a Felipe / policíacas / las películas

_____

9. el trabajo / a Angélica / aburrir / le

_____

10. la comida / italiana / encantar / a Vanessa y a mí / nos

_____

Realidades

Nombre _____

Hora _____

Capítulo 9A

Fecha _____

Practice Workbook **9A–8**

Repaso

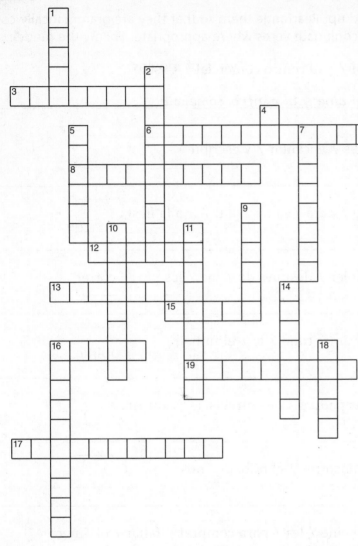

Down

1. Yo veo mis programas favoritos en el ___ cinco.
2. Es más que interesante; es ___.
4. *already*
5. No es actor, es ___.
7. No es interesante, es ___.
9. Me van a ___ zapatos. Necesito comprarlos.
10. Puedes leer las ___ o verlas en la tele.

11. _____ película ___
14. *really?*
16. A Paco le gusta el fútbol. Ve programas ___.
18. No sé mucho ___ eso.

Across

3. Cuando vas al cine, ves una ___.

6.
8. un programa en la tele que cuenta las historias románticas de la gente; la ___

12. *therefore*
13. Una comedia es ___.
15. No es actriz, es ___.
16. Los programas ___ una hora.
17. *Entre tú y yo* es un programa de ___.
19. Cuando la gente gana dinero, es un programa de ___.

Realidades A/B

Capítulo 9A

Nombre _____

Hora _____

Fecha _____

Practice Workbook **9A–9**

Organizer

I. Vocabulary

Types of television programs

_____

_____

_____

_____

_____

_____

_____

Types of movies

_____

_____

_____

_____

_____

_____

_____

Words to describe movies/programs

_____

_____

_____

_____

_____

Words to express opinions

_____

_____

_____

_____

_____

II. Grammar

1. Use _____ + _____ to say what you or others have just finished doing.

2. **Me gusta** is literally translated as "_____". So, the construction is formed by putting the _____ first, followed by the _____, and finally the _____.

Realidades A/B

Nombre _____

Hora _____

Capítulo 9B

Fecha _____

Practice Workbook **9B–1**

El laboratorio

Label the computer lab below with the appropriate words.

1. _____   4. _____

2. _____   5. _____

3. _____   6. _____

Go Online WEB CODE jcd-0911
PHSchool.com

Realidades A/B

Capítulo 9B

Nombre _____

Fecha _____

Hora _____

Practice Workbook **9B–2**

Las asociaciones

Write the words from your vocabulary that you associate with each of the following definitions.

1. Una sala de clases con muchas computadoras _____

2. Lugar para hablar con otras personas en línea _____

3. Comunicarse con otros por computadora _____

4. Lo que haces si quieres aprender más _____

5. Buscar información _____

6. Un lugar de la Red dedicado a algún tema _____

7. Hacer actividades electrónicas divertidas _____

8. Una comunicación *no* por correo electrónico _____

9. Una carta que envías para una fecha especial _____

10. Expresar y comprender ideas de otra persona _____

11. Si quieres hacer un disco compacto _____

12. Un artista puede hacerlos en la computadora _____

Realidades A/B

Capítulo 9B

Nombre _____

Hora _____

Fecha _____

Practice Workbook **9B–3**

El sitio Web

Sara has just purchased a laptop computer. She is so excited that she just has to tell her friend Ramón. In the e-mail below write the words that best complete her thoughts.

Ramón,

Ay, amigo, tienes que comprarte una computadora

_____. ¡Son los mejores juguetes del mundo!

Cuando vas de vacaciones puedes llevarla en tu mochila y

cuando estás en el hotel puedes _____ en la

Red, escribir por _____ o

_____ información de la Red. ¿Y quieres

sacar fotos? Con una cámara _____ puedes

sacarlas y ponerlas en la computadora. También puedes

mandar las fotos a otra _____ electrónica

si quieres. ¿Qué te _____? ¿Es difícil?

Puedes _____ un curso para aprender más

sobre cómo usar esta clase de cámara y cómo crear

_____ en la computadora. No debes tener

_____ de buscar información sobre

cámaras digitales porque hay muchas personas que

_____ usarlas o que escribieron unos

_____ sobre estas cámaras.

Bueno, podemos hablar más de esto _____

porque no tengo tiempo ahora. Hasta luego.

Sara

Go Online WEB CODE jcd-0912
PHSchool.com

Realidades A/B

Capítulo 9B A/B

Nombre

Fecha

Hora

Practice Workbook **9B–4**

¡Una computadora muy buena!

Your local newspaper recently ran an ad for a new computer and many of your friends bought one. Read some of the computer's capabilities in the ad below. Then, based on the information you are given about each person that bought this computer, say what he or she uses the new computer for. Follow the model.

CON LA COMPUTADORA ES POSIBLE:

- Grabar un disco compacto
- Preparar presentaciones
- Escribir por correo electrónico
- Usar una cámara digital
- Visitar salones de chat
- Navegar en la Red
- Crear documentos
- Estar en línea

Modelo A Juan le gusta bajar información.

Juan usa la computadora para estar en línea.

1. A Alejandro le gusta escribir cuentos y composiciones.

   _____

2. A Diego le gusta sacar fotos.

   _____

3. A Caridad le gusta tocar y escuchar música.

   _____

4. A Ramiro le gusta buscar los sitios Web.

   _____

5. A Esperanza le gusta conocer y hablar con otras personas.

   _____

6. A Lucita le gusta escribir tarjetas y cartas a su familia que vive en otra ciudad.

   _____

7. A Rodrigo le gusta enseñar a los niños.

   _____

Realidades **A/B**

Capítulo 9B

Nombre _____

Hora _____

Fecha _____

Practice Workbook **9B–5**

¿Pedir o servir?

A. Fill in the charts below with the present tense forms of the verbs **pedir** and **servir**.

	PEDIR	SERVIR
yo	*pido*	
tú		
él, ella, Ud.		*sirve*
nosotros		
vosotros	*pedís*	*servís*
ellos, ellas, Uds.		

B. Complete the mini-conversations below with the correct forms of **pedir** or **servir**.

1. —Cuando vas al restaurante Marino para comer, ¿qué _____ tú?

    —Normalmente _____ una ensalada y una pasta.

2. —¿Para qué _____ esto?

    —_____ para grabar discos compactos, hijo.

3. —¿Los camareros les _____ rápidamente en el restaurante Guzmán?

    —Sí, son muy trabajadores.

4. —No puedo ver esos gráficos.

    —(Nosotros) _____ ayuda, entonces.

5. —Bienvenida a la fiesta. ¿Le _____ algo?

    —Sí, un refresco, por favor.

6. —Vamos al restaurante. Esta noche ellos _____ pollo con salsa y pasta.

    —Yo siempre _____ el pollo.

7. —¿Para qué _____ el menú?

    —_____ para conocer la comida del restaurante. ¿Y qué vas a

    _____ del menú?

    —Yo siempre _____ la misma cosa. . . el bistec.

Go Online WEB CODE jcd-0913
PHSchool.com

Realidades A/B

Capítulo 9B

Nombre _____

Fecha _____

Hora _____

Practice Workbook **9B–6**

¿Saber o conocer?

A. Write either **saber** or **conocer** in the blanks under the items below.

1. Mi número de teléfono

   _____

2. Usar una computadora

   _____

3. El profesor de la clase de español

   _____

4. La película *Casablanca*

   _____

5. Leer música

   _____

6. La ciudad de Nueva York

   _____

7. Mi madre

   _____

8. Tu mejor amigo

   _____

9. Navegar en la Red

   _____

10. El sitio Web

   _____

B. Fill in the missing forms of **saber** and **conocer** in the charts below.

	SABER	CONOCER
yo		
tú		
él, ella, Ud.	*sabe*	*conoce*
nosotros		
vosotros	*sabéis*	*conocéis*
ellos, ellas, Uds.		

C. Complete the following sentences using the correct forms of **saber** or **conocer**.

1. Juan, ¿ _____ la fecha de hoy?

2. ¿Alguien _____ a un médico bueno?

3. Mis padres _____ bailar muy bien.

4. Nosotros _____ todas las palabras de la obra.

5. ¿ _____ dónde está el Museo del Prado?

Realidades **A/B**

Capítulo 9B

Nombre _____

Fecha _____

Hora _____

Practice Workbook **9B–7**

Planes para la noche

The Miranda family is planning to go out to eat. Fill in their conversation using forms of
conocer, **saber**, **pedir**, or **servir**.

PADRE: Vamos al restaurante Vista del Mar. ¿Lo _____ Uds.? Me gusta

mucho.

TERESA: Yo no lo _____ pero _____ dónde está. ¡Quiero ir

a ese restaurante!

TOMÁS: Por supuesto que _____ dónde está, Tere, el nombre es Vista del Mar.

TERESA: Sí. ¿_____ Uds. que tienen el mejor pescado de la ciudad?

Es muy sabroso.

MADRE: ¿Y ellos _____ otra comida también?

TERESA: Yo no _____ . ¿Sabes tú, Tomás?

TOMÁS: Sí. Allí _____ mucha comida rica.

PADRE: Yo _____ el pescado porque me encanta.

TOMÁS: Sí, me encanta el pescado también.

TERESA: Es verdad Tomás, pero siempre _____ la misma cosa cuando

comemos pescado.

PADRE: Por eso vamos a este restaurante. Puedes _____ de todo y va a ser

sabrosísimo.

TERESA: ¡Yo quiero _____ ese restaurante!

MADRE: Pues, estamos de acuerdo. Vamos a Vista del Mar.

Go Online WEB CODE jcd-0915
PHSchool.com

Realidades **A/B**

Capítulo 9B

Nombre _____

Hora _____

Fecha _____

Practice Workbook **9B–8**

Repaso

Down

1.

2. El cliente ___ un té helado porque tiene calor.

3. Voy a visitar Nueva York porque quiero ___ la.

4. ___ un disco compacto

6. Los estudiantes hacen un ___ del presidente Lincoln.

8. Quiero escribirte una carta. ¿Cuál es tu ___ electrónica?

9. Yo escribo por ___ electrónico.

11. Estoy en línea. Quiero ___ en ___.

12. *song;* la ___

13. El ___ Web para este libro es *PHSchool.com.*

14. No tengo ese programa. Lo voy a ___ de la Red.

16. Necesito ___ información para mi informe.

18. La artista sabe muy bien hacer ___ en la computadora.

19. Necesito una computadora que puede ___ documentos.

21. *slide;* la ___

Across

1. Quiero ___ un curso.

5. No debes tener ___ de la tecnología.

7. Para navegar en la Red, hay que estar ___ ___.

10. Si quieres hablar con personas inmediatamente, vas a un ___ de chat.

13. ¿Para qué ___?

15. *to communicate (with)*

17. Mi amiga me escribió una ___.

20. No me gusta hablar por teléfono. Me gusta hablar ___ ___ ___.

22. Voy a la escuela porque quiero ___ cómo hacer cosas.

23. Vamos al ___ para usar las computadoras de la escuela.

24. la computadora ___

Realidades A/B

Capítulo 9B

Nombre _____

Fecha _____

Hora _____

Practice Workbook **9B–9**

Organizer

I. Vocabulary

Words to talk about the Web

_____

_____

_____

_____

Words to name other electronics

_____

_____

_____

_____

Verbs related to online activities

_____

_____

_____

_____

_____

_____

II. Grammar

1. The present tense of **pedir** is:

   _____ _____

   _____ _____

   _____ _____

   The present tense of **servir** is:

   _____ _____

   _____ _____

   _____ _____

2. Use the verb _____ for information or activities that you know. Use the verb _____ to talk about familiarity with people, places, or things.

Go Online WEB CODE jcd-0916
PHSchool.com